First published in 2019
by Propolis Books
The Book Hive,
53 London Street,
Norwich, NR2 1HL

cover design and photography by Niki Medlik
at **studio medlikova**
www.medlikova.com
with thanks to Harry Malt
for hand-drawn type & illustrations
www.harrymalt.co.uk

A CIP record for this book
is available from the British Library

Printed and bound by TJ International, Padstow, Cornwall

www.propolisbooks.co.uk

Jeremy Page

NEW YORK TO CALIFORNIA

A journey across the East of England

looking for the not quite visible

propolis

"Don't you start nothin you can't stop."
Ron Reptile, 1993

"But I'm not *equalised!*"
Anon

Contents

for my mother

PART ONE

DEFYING THE CURVE

New York

Standing at the junction between Dogdyke Road and Langrick Road, in a landscape that looked like corrugated metal beaten flat, I stared at the village sign and couldn't quite believe what I was seeing. There wasn't much around me – a few houses, no shop, and only a single bus stop where a minibus was due to arrive at seven minutes past every hour, en route from Lincoln to Boston. On the other side of the road was a cabbage field. I listened to a tractor ploughing in the distance, and then looked at the sign again, because this tiny village, in a forgotten corner of the Lincolnshire fens, is called New York.

But it's certainly not America. Compared to the other one, it's a very small apple.

I didn't know much about this New York, other than its name, that it has bungalows instead of skyscrapers, and that it would be the beginning of my journey towards the equally small village of California, on the Norfolk coast – noted for its chalet park and amusements arcade – exactly one hundred miles away from where I stood. And I knew one other thing. Sixty years ago, my mother had a boyfriend here. Behind one of those double-glazed windows was the home I might have been born into.

I'm in my forties. About twice as old as my mother was when she last came here to see the boyfriend who didn't become my father. While I'm at the right age for a midlife reappraisal, the more obvious temptation might have been to fly to America, buy a motorbike and ride it coast to coast from the more famous New York to the more famous California. But for a variety of reasons I'm not doing that. It's difficult to explain, but something has stirred in me, a feeling deep in my bones that I can only liken to a sense of a migration needing to occur. I've heard this happens in eels. They live for many years in the calm waters of their chosen ponds and marshes, growing comfortable and lazy and complacent with life and then, all of a sudden – due to some alignment of the stars perhaps, or chemical release in their DNA – they know they have to move. Migration calls them to make a difficult journey, to abandon the luxuries of their life and to return home. The eel gets the call, and pursues this migration with admirable determination. It decides that it will never eat again, but will live purely off its own bodily reserves. On a moonlit night the eel leaves its pond, and slides with resolve through the reed beds. If it arrives at the wall of a sluice it will not give up, but will wriggle up the bank, cross a tarmac road, slide down through the grass on the other side, and with unerring skill, continue its watery route. It slips in through the reeds and swims like a single thread of the river, heading for the ocean, and will never see land again.

Eels, like me, share an East Anglian upbringing, so I feel I understand this particular impulse well enough. I too have had the call, and have chosen to follow the route my family took across East Anglia a generation before me. So I stood at the crossroads, on a bright sunny morning in mid-June, waiting for my travel companion to arrive – a man called Heath. I was always intending to do this journey by myself, but at the last minute Heath got in touch with me and said he'd like to come along, for at least some part of it. I wasn't sure at first. I don't know that much about him, other than he's a bit older than me, he lives in Cambridge, has had a number of changes of career, and once invented a fairly well used kitchen gadget. We've been in e-mail correspondence for several years, over various bits of research, and I can tell you he likes to observe the things just below the surface – the not quite visible part of life. I decided it might be good to have him join me. He looks a bit like the actor Ian Holm.

He's also very punctual. At 9:55am precisely I saw him cycling towards me on the Dogdyke Road, wobbling slightly in the saddle. He appeared like a moving dot against the landscape, much like Omar Sharif's appearance in the iconic scene in *Lawrence of Arabia*. Instead of desert, Heath was of course surrounded by flat agricultural land. Even from a few hundred yards away I could see the level of concentration he was putting in to maintaining a straight line, on a road that had no bends.

When he reached me, my first surprise was that Heath had brought a dog with him, which hadn't been part of our agreement. He set the dog down on the pavement: a tan-coloured whippet, with a tail that looked like it would be permanently curled between its hind legs.

'You look worried,' Heath said. 'But no need – the dog's going to run alongside the bikes, and when he gets tired he can sit in this.' He tapped a basket fixed above his rear mudguard. 'Besides,' he added, 'Half-Shandy will keep us sane.' He gave me a wink, as if sanity might be one of our concerns. The dog looked up at him, hearing his name mentioned, then sat on the kerb quivering.

We started at New York's road sign, viewing it from the nearby bus stop. *New York* was spelt out in large bright letters. It stood in front of the cabbage field. Above the name was a second sign, more dominant and this one as golden as an egg yolk, with a 40mph speed limit written inside a red circle.

Heath wondered why there was no graffiti on the sign: 'Surely the name New York needs to have "The Other One," written just below?'

The tractor I'd been listening to began to work its way along the edge of the cabbage field. It reached the end of a row, then turned. Heath thought we should split the village between us. He suggested we take an hour, but we both instinctively looked at our watches, and agreed half an hour might do it.

'Do you want to do the Langrick Road, or Dogdyke Road?' I asked.

'Let's toss for it.' He took out a coin.

'Heads,' I called, while it was still flipping in the air.

Walking back to the crossroads, I wondered which one of these houses might have been the one my mother's boyfriend lived in. Before I came here I asked her which one it was and she said she couldn't remember. It had green curtains, was the only clue she could give. Green curtains, sixty years ago. Anything else, I asked? A pond.

Further down the road, Heath was looking at the notice board outside the village hall. I thought about the route we'd chosen to do from New York to California, knowing that I also had a secret migratory agenda that I hadn't entirely told him. I wasn't sure what I should be looking for in New York. Perhaps something tongue-in-cheek, like a miniature Chrysler building set beside a garden path, or a Statue of Liberty bumper sticker on a tractor's trailer. I stepped into the road and for the two minutes I spent there, nothing passed me in either direction. It all looked pretty deserted.

As I walked up the Langrick Road, the only business I found was one called *Concrete Gardens*, which made various ornamental figurines and urns. Scattered around the front lawn were several examples of what they were selling – Doric columns and birdbaths and a nymph standing in the long grass exposing a single bared breast. Leaning against the gatepost was a concrete Botticelli's Venus, minus her head, which didn't seem a good advert for their workmanship. Surely they'd considered moulding miniature skyscrapers to sell along the roadside, with *Made in New York* stamped on each one? It seemed like a moneymaking no-brainer.

I read the house names, hoping to spot a *Manhattan View* or *Little Rockefeller* among them. But to no avail. What I found instead was a house named *First Bungalow* and, a few steps further, another named *The Bungalow*. The two houses looked similar, and there must have been moments of confusion between them. I imagined someone giving surreal directions: 'I live up there, in the bungalow, not the first bungalow, but First Bungalow. It's the second one you get to.' Further along the same road I came to a house named *Capri*, which also seemed an odd choice for a name, because its address must have been something like: *Capri, New York, Lincolnshire* – three different destinations that very few people had been to in any one life.

Frankly, I already felt frustrated, and Sinatra's *New York, New York* was beginning to go round and round in my head in a kind of demented jingle, which didn't help. I suppose I'd expected to find more irony, that there might be a grocer's called *The Big Apple* – a gag clearly worth making – or a gent's outfitters called *Times Squire*. A souvenir shop would have helped, selling postcards of *Greetings from New York* mocked up in a 1970s razzmatazz font, and instead of the letters being filled with views of the Empire State Building and Statue of Liberty, there would be images of the bus stop, village hall, and a tractor crossing the main road. Or there might have been one of those eccentrically charming museums you can still find in British villages, where an enthusiastically warm old man will sit you in front of an eight minute video presentation of local history.

Instead it looked like a very ordinary fenland village, which you could pass through without any reason to stop. No shop, no pub, and set in a landscape so flat the roads had no curves, no reason to slow you down. The village had no capture to it, as though it was meant to vanish at every angle. Before even starting my journey, I felt I'd lost my way.

I walked up to the bus shelter and wrote down the names of all the stops on the C17 route:

Lincoln city bus station, Washingborough Road, Branston Cross Roads, Potterhanworth Memorial, Nocton Hall Gates, Dunston Church, Metheringham Co-Op, Metheringham Rail Station, Blankney Barff, Martin Church, Kirkstead Bridge, Woodhall Spa, Tattershall, Thorpe Gartree School, Tattershall Market Place, Coningsby Community Centre, Dogdyke, Hawthorn Hill, Scrub Hill, New York, Hundlehouses, Gipsey Bridge, Langrick, Anton's Gowt, Cowbridge, Pilgrim Hospital, Boston Bus Station.

The names read like a mantra, covering the distance from Lincoln to Boston. The stops sounded windswept, placed on empty roads or next to a gate or Co-Op or community centre. Those bus shelters must be draughty places, I thought, with a chilly bench and a long view across flat fields, and not much to do other than try to spot the tiny minibus that would eventually materialise in the distance. Waiting for public transport in the fens must be a meditative experience, one where you would watch the journey coming towards you long before the bus actually arrived with a warm shake of its engine and the hydraulic sigh of its opening door. I wondered whether my mother had ever waited at this bus stop, and imagined her quietly looking out over the fen, balancing her options against the spirit level of the horizon.

I noticed two of the bus stops were named after hills – Hawthorn Hill and Scrub Hill – but looking beyond the sign I could only see perfect flatness. I suspected a rise of ten or twenty feet might be enough to be called a hill, and that this kind of landscape needed to be judged by its own rules. Reading the list again, I tried to imagine I was from the village of Dogdyke. What it would feel like? *Where are you from? I'm from Dogdyke, have you heard of it? Don't think so. Right, it's a small crossroads in the Lincolnshire fens.* It sounded exotic. And it sounded as though I didn't really know what I was talking about.

Down the road I could see Heath examining a pebbledash wall. Half-Shandy was milling about on the pavement behind him, walking on tiptoes, sniffing something on the kerb. Heath was really staring at that wall, as though he'd just fallen there from outer space. He was leaning forward at the pebbledash like it was a grainy photo of the moon's surface, his hands crossed behind his back in the manner of a school teacher.

'I found a house called *Brooklyn*,' he said, a little triumphantly, when I reached him.

'Good, you had more luck than me. I haven't really found that much.' But I told him about *Capri*, in *New York*, in *Lincolnshire*. He looked troubled by that. He couldn't understand that at all. Then I told him about the naming of the bungalows.

'Adding those to one I found,' he said, 'that's two "The Bungalows" and one "First Bungalow."'

'In New York, all within a hundred yards.'

'Incredible.'

We'd found very little to go on. New York had thwarted us by being quietly absent, and the journey ahead seemed like it would be a lot more concealed than I imagined. California now seemed a long way away, I thought to myself, and felt guilty for inviting Heath and his dog along on a journey that already appeared absurd. If only we'd found something startling here. There should have been B&Bs offering weekend breaks in New York. The business opportunities seemed endless for a kind of ironic tourism that hadn't been discovered yet. I imagined couples turning up here and, on the second day of walking up and down the street, wondering whether they were now properly mad. Irony is a kind of empty calorie that ultimately can't sustain you for more than a few hours. And then I wondered was I being just that: an ironic tourist? It seemed an ill fit for what I was trying to do here – journey across East Anglia and discover it afresh. I'm not here to write a travelogue, I reminded myself. I'm here with an open mind, setting out to follow a particular route but equally happy to lose myself among the detours. If New York has not entirely revealed itself, then that's something I should accept. There will be chances elsewhere, and true inspiration tends to occur when you don't go looking for it. I'm here to follow the stories I remember and those my family have passed down, and place them on a route that starts in the fen and ends at the North Sea. Two watery landscapes in a very watery region. There are many other ways of measuring a journey than it just being the shortest distance between two points, and it was these I wanted to find.

So I left New York, feeling slightly baffled, but quietly affectionate for a place that might have been – had my mother stayed – my home. And I decided that when I got back I'd mock up one of those fabulous razzmatazz font postcards for it.

To Anton's Gowt

Leaving New York, we set off towards California on a perfectly straight road, stretched across the fen like a fallen ribbon. Heath cycled in front, with Half-Shandy just behind his back wheel, trotting on tiptoes. In the distance, pools of mirage rose from the tarmac, lifting the white lines painted along the verge and making them dance in the air like bunting. It was a warm day, the sky was pale blue, and the long views of the fens on both sides of the road seemed to pull at me like a vacuum. The world looked unmade all round – scraped down to a bare level.

Half my family came from the fens; I should have this ruler-flat landscape in my bones, and should have felt reassured, freewheeling, going down that road in a land without slopes. But perhaps that kind of reassurance only comes if your whole life has been spent here. My mother's cousin, for instance – who has hardly left the fen she was born on – was once taken on a day trip to the hilly area of the Lincolnshire Wolds, almost, it seems, as an experiment. That day, she was let out of the car, and she apparently laughed and slipped and fell over a hundred times, purely because the slopes played havoc with her balance. That's a woman who knows about flatness, and to her a world with hills is strange and untrustworthy. I don't share her particular worldview, but I do have a root in this flatland, and maybe it's this family history that has given me the posture of walking with a straight back, tall as a fenland poplar. And possibly it's my family's hundreds of years of fenland living that has given me the ability to judge the level of a shelf with spot on accuracy. Yes, the fens must have left their imprint in the DNA but, nonetheless, cycling towards Anton's Gowt, and faced with this relentless flatness, I wanted to bend the geometry of the landscape around me, pulling up parts of the fields with strings to give it a shape. I wanted hills and valleys, rivers and meadows, and trees along a ridge.

My family were farmers, north east of Boston, and by the time my mother was born they'd already moved off the land, their smallholding making way for the kind of supersized agriculture that has now taken over. The farm itself was bulldozed, to make way for larger fields, and when my mother once tried to find where the building had been, all she discovered were a few loose bricks left behind in the soil. Generations of her family living and working the land had been removed from the map, and she stood there with a single brick in her hand, holding on to all that was left. She put it in a carrier bag, thinking that if she didn't do anything, it would sink into the soil and be lost forever. And before she left, she took a moment to reflect on something her father had once told her – that when he was a child he used to be pushed into a hole under the kitchen floor as a punishment. And be left there. Somewhere near her, or perhaps under her very feet, was that particular space, now sealed up and filled with soil.

Ahead of me Heath suddenly stopped, got off his bike, and disappeared into one of the hedges. I drew alongside and watched bits of him as he tugged at the branches. There was a snap and he fell back out.

'Ah-ha!' he said, brandishing a Y-shaped twig of hazel. 'I have found us a dowsing rod. To help with our navigation.' He wiggled it at me, then began stripping the leaves.

'Will it work?'

'No idea. But Lincolnshire's riddled with water – it's bound to pick up on something.'

Water divining, I thought. I'll add it to the list – because previous conversations have taught me that Heath has many pet subjects he likes to go on about. This list includes: nuclear fission, typographical fonts, cheese, the poor design of modern cars, dahlias, the golden age of post-war rocketry, bluegrass music, sushi, gravity and card tricks. He's eclectic, and often surprising. There are only a few subjects I've never heard him talk about. Among them are football, online shopping and foreign holidays, which may help give a sense of the kind of man he is and the way he likes to live his life.

While writing this book I discovered a Sutton's Seeds tin from the 1950s full of my grandfather's photos, and I have included several of them among my own pictures as a kind of dual commentary on the journey. Here, in a photo taken in 1927, he captured a view of 'a windswept fenland drove.' In fact, those are the words he wrote on the back of the picture, in fine copperplate handwriting. It looks very much like the road Heath and I cycled down from New York. I don't know the precise location, but like to think that even though most of my grandfather's adult life was spent in the fens, there were still moments when the sheer flatness, the distance and the relentless geometry were strong enough to make him stop, look, and reach for his camera.

We turned off the road near Gypsy Bridge to take a long dog-leg towards Boston, on a narrow lane squeezed between hawthorn hedges. Beyond the hedges there were rapeseed fields, in full flower, and the pollen gave off an overpowering smell of fish. A sickly yellow pallor seemed to be hanging in the air, giving the road a jaundiced, oppressive quality. Heath stopped to put his already tired dog in its mudguard basket, and I cycled on in silence. When I looked back he was fussing with the basket, and I saw him wave me on.

After a couple of miles I reached Anton's Gowt which – although it sounds like a medical complaint – is where the River Witham makes a sudden elbow-angled turn towards the south east. I leant my bike against a municipal sign warning against the dangers of swimming, and looked down at the river. My eel-sense of migration picked up the scent of water, and knew the Witham was a special river for my family. My mother grew up on its bank, and as a child would cycle up to this spot at Anton's Gowt each Saturday, to visit a couple of goats. She would bring them carrots and swedes, and during the two-and-a-half miles from her house in Boston, those vegetables would jump and dance in the basket as her bike rode the bumps of the river path. At Anton's Gowt she would lean her bike against the goat pen and greet her friends, tethered, here at the outer limits of her known world. Below her, the calm dark river water would slowly pass by. She would look into the goat's ungodly eyes as they ate her vegetable gifts, and they would look back at her without recognition or gratitude. All would be still, apart from the relentless chewing of those teeth, the swallowing of the cud, the regurgitation and the chewing and the second swallowing. Those goats, with their ancient wise faces, must have felt like gatekeepers. Beyond Anton's Gowt her world was totally untravelled.

Among my grandfather's photos in the seed tin were a few taken by my father, including a picture of two white goats eating grass along a fenland riverbank, taken somewhere near Spalding in the early '50s. Unlike the photos taken by my grandfather, my father's ones can't keep a level horizon. Perhaps that's a clue that he, like me, felt the urge to make slopes in a land where there weren't any. It's a strange photo, with lines converging at a vanishing point on its horizon, which is something you face regularly in the fens. These are not my mother's goats, but the way they stand on the verge between the road and ditch suggests they too were sentries of a different border – possibly marking the point where my father's own journeys needed to turn back.

Heath looked flustered when he finally rode up, and was clearly preoccupied by the mechanisms of his bike. Something was sticking or squeaking or hadn't been oiled properly. I noticed Half-Shandy was hanging his head languidly out of the basket fixed above the mudguard. The dog looked exhausted.

'So,' he called, 'we are approaching the first stop on our transcontinental journey. Boston, home of the Tea Party, Red Sox, and Harvard. How far is it?'

I pointed. 'A couple of miles along the river.'

He pointed his hazel dowsing rod towards the river, to see if it twitched.

'Any luck?' I asked.

'Inconclusive.' He dropped it onto the grass.

'Right,' he said, raising his hand to quell an issue which was not, in fact, in the air. 'You want to see where your mother grew up, and don't need me holding you back. I shall take the road to the Stump and meet you there. You'll be on the river path.'

'Thanks, Heath.'

'Nice spot, Anton's Gowt,' he said.

Heath pushed off on his bike, wobbling in the saddle as he tried to get his foot on the pedal. He is many things, but born cyclist he's not.

'At the Stump, then,' he called back, unbalanced.

Boston

As I cycled along the riverbank, I thought of how my mother had once seen a German bomber, a Heinkel, flying down this same stretch of river, following its course back to the Wash, the North Sea, and the distant coast of Germany. According to her, the plane had a mottled dogfish-skin camouflage, was streaked with exhaust burns on its engines, and had a shot-through tail, giving it a ragged feathery look. This lonesome bomber flew low enough to clip the chimney pots, its engines thundering past while short staccato bursts of gunfire came from its turrets, as it prepared to let loose any remaining bombs onto the sleepy Lincolnshire town of Boston. But my mother's most lingering memory wasn't of the bombs or the machine gun fire. What struck her most was seeing her father throwing himself flat on the front lawn and, as the Heinkel roared overhead, how he'd suddenly burst out laughing. Because further down the riverbank the plane was now shooting at a friend of his, deliberately making him dance, and while his friend was hopping around among the bullets, he was protecting himself by frantically turning up his jacket collar.

With a little effort I could almost smell this Heinkel. When it's necessary to imagine the big, it's often best to start with the small, and here I focused on the sensation in the pilot's wrists as he held the plane level, exhausted, from gripping the steering column through the night. A few hours earlier, he must have seen the land below him lighting up with flames, and those wrists must have felt the strangely buoyant uplift as each bomb tipped out. Those scenes from the bombing raid would be consigned to a specific part of the pilot's memory – the place where unimaginable sights should be filed away. Those memories might have to be denied at some later point in his life, because they don't bear scrutiny in a normal world. That will be faced in time to come. But here, flying low over the river, I imagine the German pilot would be feeling relieved to be on the way home. He'd survived the night, and now sunlight was flooding into the cockpit, diluting the smells of cordite and axle grease and hot electricity. A radio was playing Vera Lynn, picked up on the British Home Service, because the bomber had no need for concealment anymore, and the sound of the song was giving him an incongruous sense of goodwill towards the countryside speeding by. Chimney pots and tiled roofs and carefully tended vegetable patches rushing underneath, as familiar as the flatlands of Lower Saxony or Schleswig-Holstein. And as he followed the River Witham, seeing the sunlight flash off the wings, perhaps there was a shared laugh among the airmen – when they saw the dancing man who'd turned his jacket collar up to protect himself from machine gun fire.

And I like to think that my grandfather, also laughing, might have caught the eye of the passing German pilot and, together, they'd shared an impossible – never to be repeated or owned up to – wink.

I reached Witham Bank East where, in the small flat-fronted house facing the river, my mother grew up. Here, at the last stretch of wild riverbank before the town began, I saw the small sandy inlet where my brother and I used to spend our weekends dragging weed from the river with a couple of sticks. The clumps of weed would deflate as the water drained out, and it would be followed by a miracle – because some of those dark green stems would begin to move, to wriggle and twist, transforming before our eyes into small eels and elvers, like so many Aaron's rods turning into snakes. Even though the eels seemed blind and faceless, each had a nose for water, and as we watched they would return to the river by direct paths, as if their bodies were liquid ribbons of the river itself, flowing downhill, returning to the sea. It's taken me forty years to fully understand those eels and their instinct to migrate. But here I was, on that same bank, feeling the urge myself. Go back, find where you came from, it's time to return.

The house had been repainted, the slates on its roof replaced, and the privet hedge round the front garden had grown taller. But I looked first to the bottom left window, because that was where my brother and I used to spend our weekends, sleeping on a pair of single beds on opposite sides of the room, both of us pressed down with a suffocating strata of our grandmother's blankets. It was a cold room forty years ago, barely furnished, unused when we weren't staying, and those beds were icy whatever the season. And as I looked at the window, I sensed that a part of me was still in that room, and always would be, sliding legs into a cold damp bed, falling asleep with a view of the river outside.

The house used to be full of knickknacks from my grandmother's Welsh childhood, covering the surfaces like crystals growing in a geode. There were carved mahogany lions on the TV, ceramic thimbles on the shelves, polished horse brasses on the mantelpiece, and tapestries in the fireplace of Welsh women wearing tall strange black hats. Where was my grandmother's own tall black hat, I used to wonder? Was it in a cupboard? Was she from a long line of Welsh witches? Could she turn frogs into toads? The dark kitchen table was tiny, and as you slid your way along the bench on one side, a lace cloth would drag, disturbing the symmetry of the woven placemats. A fire grate next to the table had a ridge of dust along each bar. I remember the drop in temperature as I stepped down into my mother's bedroom from the landing, how the light in there was whiter than in the living room, which had the river's green glow in it, and the small cupboard room above the stairs with its window overlooking the Witham. A room I would love now, but ignored then. Time would pass slowly in there, in rhythm with the river's flow outside.

My grandmother's bedroom was out of bounds, but we would sneak in there to marvel at the automatic Teasmade by her bed, which had elaborate buttons and wires surrounding a clock. It looked like someone else had crept in and put a time bomb there. Who was it, my brother and I used to ask? Who wanted to blow her up?

In the back garden I now saw newly laid paving stones, and I missed the old mossy path that had been there, and the little round pond where I always believed – for some reason – my mother used to wash her hair, and the dark shape of the garage that had once stood there. That garage in particular had been a mysterious place. A terrifically heavy length of felted curtain had hung as a doorway and, beyond it, standing in the shadows, was my nana's tan-coloured Mini, which smelt of old metal and leather and oil. Pulling that curtain aside – thick as a Russian greatcoat – was a theatrical experience, and always felt like the crossing of one of childhood's enigmatic frontiers.

While I was at the garden gate, a woman came out of the house. She said good morning and I explained how I used to know this place. She invited me in, to take a look around. Behind her, I could see a glimpse of new kitchen cabinets, and there was a smell of washing powder coming from the doorway that had never belonged there. I declined the invitation, knowing that memories have a surprisingly fragile quality; return to a room where they were formed, and they can easily fall apart.

I hurried along the riverbank to Boston's one and only skyscraper – the Stump – Britain's tallest church tower. It looms above the rest of the town with extra impact because the surrounding land is so flat. Half-Shandy was tied to a foot scraper, next to Heath's bike. I pushed open the heavy oak door and stepped into the cool of the church, with my gaze immediately drawn upwards to the nave's ceiling, which was startlingly lofty, like a new gilded and embossed sky.

The aisle was made of smoothly polished tombstones, seamlessly joined with one another like a patchwork of the dead. They were granite or basalt, and were impenetrably dark and solid, yet the centuries had softened the edges of each one, giving them a semi-melted appearance. The sunlight glanced off them with a waxy shine, where the inscriptions had been worn away by the hundreds of years of shoes and boots that had walked over them. The living, erasing the dead. The wearing down of these tough igneous rocks by this soft erosion felt revelatory. It allowed a glimpse into time that was more like a depth than a direction.

At the far end of the church I saw Heath crouching among the choir stalls. He was sketching the famous misericord carving of a choir master spanking the bum of a choir boy.

'Religion has much to answer for,' he said, when I approached. 'And did you know Reverend John Cotton's sermons could go on for five hours?'

'John Cotton?'

'Went to the Massachusetts Bay Colony with the rest of the puritans, aboard the *Griffin*, in the wake of the other two boats from Boston, the *Arabella* and the *Mayflower*.'

'I know about the *Mayflower*.'

'Yes, and you've heard of America, I presume,' Heath said. Like all men with a good general knowledge, he can be impatient at times.

Then he announced, quite randomly, that he'd reached the age where his footwear *must always* be comfortable: 'I will never again wear shoes that haven't got cushioned soles,' he said. 'Plantar fasciitis stalks men like me. It hides in leather shoes. These –' he pointed, accusingly '– have had their day.'

Embarking on a hundred-mile journey in poor shoes is a good example of the way Heath thinks. He gets caught up in other issues, and can easily leave his flat in a pair of slippers and pyjamas, holding a letter that needs a stamp. This has actually happened. He has told me.

Outside the Stump, I tried to show Heath the cracked paving slab my grandmother always claimed was split in two by a man jumping to his death from the tower. Bothered by his shoe crisis, Heath joined me half-heartedly in the search, but it was clear that since my childhood, a repaving scheme had covered the area, removing all trace of this particular story.

All thoughts of exploring Boston were put to one side as Heath led the way to find himself new shoes. In the marketplace, we walked past the Assembly Rooms where my mum and dad first met each other at a dance in the 1950s. To emphasise his discomfort, Heath was now putting on a limp. I kept my thoughts to myself, imagining my dad's Brylcreamed hair swept back from his youthful forehead, and my mother's enthusiastic dancing, and me and my brother in a preborn universe, keeping our fingers crossed that my father's chat-up lines would work. Walking by, I imagined my mother still up there in the ballroom, dancing, her jig always a little bit close to a Charleston for a credible '50s rock n' roll. On the far side of the marketplace, we passed Oldrids department store, where my mother bought her wedding dress, and where now – in a peculiar parting of time – a wedding dress was still on display in a first floor window, advertising itself to the new generation of couples getting it together in Boston's marketplace.

Heath swooped into Shoe Zone and immediately came to a halt in front of a bewildering wall of trainers. I stopped at the doorway, suspecting he had at least an hour's worth of opinions to voice about shoe design, and told him I'd come back in a while.

My grandfather's photo of Boston Haven, taken in 1927. Age has given this photo a luminous quality, like Vermeer's painting of Delft in 1661.

In the last ten years, Boston has changed more than in the previous thousand. It is now classed as one of England's most multinational towns, due to the influx of agricultural labourers from Eastern Europe and the Baltic States, yet is also known as The Brexit Capital of England, due to its Leave vote of 75.6% being the highest recorded in the 2016 referendum. Among other dubious accolades, Boston has been labelled the Laziest Town in Britain (due to its percentage of benefit claimants), the Most Divided Town in Britain and, in 2007, the Fattest Town in Britain, with 31% of adults being classed as obese. In 2015, Murder Capital of Britain was added to its growing list. Clearly something has been going on here since my visits as a child. People were getting lazy, then fat, then angry, and then they were killing each other.

Almost by accident I emerged next to the park where, when he was seven or eight, my brother was bullied by a ten-year-old girl. As I looked at the same set of swings and roundabout, I remembered the way my brother had started laughing at a joke the girl had told, before she turned smartly on him with the unforgettable line:

'Are you laughing at me because I've got a hairy back?'

He had no response to that, so she started punching and punching him until I sat on the ground and cried my heart out. It was one of those injustices of childhood that define right-from-wrong and, only now, forty years later, am I beginning to suspect that perhaps there was more to it than I believed. Perhaps my brother *did* laugh at her because she had a hairy back.

The hairy-backed-girl may have missed a trick, because there's a tradition of physical oddness in Lincolnshire as being something that can earn you a living, especially among the men, who seem to revel in exhibiting themselves. In 1809 Daniel Lambert, self-certified as the heaviest man in history till that time, toured Lincolnshire in a specially built carriage, charging a shilling a view. He had once fought a bear for money, and for many years exhibited himself in Piccadilly, at one point alongside Józef Boruwłaski, the three-foot-three inch self-styled Tom Thumb, and last of Europe's court dwarfs. Lambert weighed fifty-two stone, had a waist of nine-foot-four inches, and was buried in an elm coffin over four-feet wide. Another famous exhibitionist who ended up in Lincolnshire was the disgraced Vicar of Stiffkey, Harold Davidson, known as the *prostitutes' padre*. After delivering his Sunday sermon in North Norfolk, he would hotfoot it to London to spend his weeks in Soho's clubs, claiming he was: 'saving the souls of fallen women.' Pull the other one, was the general response, and his antics became a national scandal. After being defrocked, his final years were spent sitting in a barrel on Skegness' seafront, protesting his innocence. My grandmother once saw Davidson in his barrel. That day, he was selling signed photos and generally ranting about being a wronged man, and how he still had much to do in the alleyways of Soho. She stood in front of him, listened to what he had to say, and wasn't impressed. Dirty bugger, is what she said to him, apparently. Other acts of his were to sit in a freezer, or – alternately – a glass-fronted oven while a mechanised devil prodded him with a pitchfork. In the evenings – to earn a bit of extra cash – he performed as part of Captain Fred Rye's animal show, where he would enter a lion's den to administer a sermon.

On 28th July 1937, he entered the lions' cage, in full vicar's regalia, to give his sermon to Freddie and Toto, when Freddie suddenly attacked and killed him. The vicar was given a celebrity's funeral, after which Freddie the lion became a new must-see act, as:

> 'The Actual Lion that Mauled and Caused the
> Death of the Ex-Rector of Stiffkey.'

But perhaps the strangest of all of the men who have exhibited themselves in Lincolnshire was one who used to loiter around Boston's marketplace in the 1950s. According to my father, who often used to see him, this man's head was so large he had to support it at all times with his hands, and would stand in the marketplace frightening the children. Not only that, but he would brag that he'd already sold his overlarge head to Boston's Pilgrim Hospital, for research purposes after he died. The Man Who Sold His Head briefly became a local attraction, known for his strangeness, appearing in my dad's and my grandmother's memories of the town, although it should be noted that while my father has – to this day – retained a residual sense of fear of this man, this bogeyman from his youth, my grandmother always regarded The Man Who Sold His Head as a fairly unremarkable sight. My grandmother was that sort of woman; she preferred things that were more grotesque than that. For instance, when I was young she used to tell me – with undue relish – about a woman she'd known in Boston who'd been standing by the side of the road when a bus caught her and dragged her under its wheels. The woman was crushed with such force that her eyes popped out, and together they shot across the pavement, hitting a butcher's window before sliding slowly down the glass. I used to listen to that story, horrified, both by the image of those eyes slipping down past the liver and chipolatas, and also at the amount of devilish enjoyment my grandmother took in telling it.

I recently asked my mother if the story was true. 'Miss Claypole, her name was,' she replied. 'She lived with Miss Haslam, my chemistry teacher.'

'Did her eyes really shoot out of her head?'

'Doubt it. And there never was a butcher's there. It was a shoe shop.'

But for me, all these years later, every shop window in Boston still has a residual trace of eyeballs sliding down the glass.

A photo of Boston women, up to mischief, making up stories. It was taken by my grandfather in 1953, probably at the Baptist Hall. I like to think my grandfather sprang up in front of them, camera in hand, attracted to the way they were sitting with their legs crossed, and a rising line of pure white scones that gives the image an almost perfect composition.

A Black Dog in Fosdyke

As we cycled out of Boston, my eel-sense felt troubled by what I'd encountered. There'd been remnants of my family and the stories they'd handed down to me, but also a reminder that my family had vanished from this place. All of them gone, migrating towards other parts of East Anglia, suggesting this empty fen landscape ultimately had no hold. How can you form an attachment, or a sense of home, I thought, where there's only flatness around you, nothing to attach to, and a horizon that seems to urge you towards escape? I looked around me, as we cycled down the main road, with agricultural lorries hurtling past us every twenty-five seconds or so, feeling the air itself was filled with a sense of restlessness, and that it would be usual here to dream about other places – places that had more to grasp on to than flat earth and distant views.

We branched off, taking the back road through the villages of Wyberton, Kirton and Sutterton. My father used to cycle this way with his best friend Brib, making intricate books of photos and hand drawn maps as they went along. I thought of the ticking of their wheels along this same stretch of road and, a generation before them, the ticking of my great uncle's three-wheeler as he delivered churns of milk from his farm to the local dairies.

In Kirton we stopped outside the laboratories on Wilmington Road where my mother was once a soil scientist, and where my grandfather was Head of Agriculture. He was a fast driver, and regularly smashed his car into the gateposts as he turned into the car park. My mother says she would be sitting in the soil lab at the back of the building when there'd be a huge crash and the other scientists would merely say: 'here he comes,' without so much as glancing up from their microscopes.

The laboratories, the gateposts, everything had gone. Around me, in the flat fen, it briefly felt as though this was a landscape where everything had been dismantled and taken away. Buildings, trees, people, whole family histories, all packed up and carted off.

But there was something undeniably remarkable about this landscape, too. My eyesight felt pulled towards the horizon in every direction. There, the edge of the world was a simple, brutally flat line. I experienced this pull – towards distances – and it made me feel stretched and yet curiously without substance, at its centre. Above me, the dome of the sky seemed bigger and more present than I was used to. I recognised its patterns of cloud and light, but felt it had an extra dimension too, an extra depth where the sky was a slightly altered element. It pressed down on me with its enormity, but made me feel a little weightless, also.

Eleven miles out of Boston the A17 looped on a bypass round the small village of Fosdyke, as it crossed Holland Fen. This was the place where, one night in the late '70s, the Mini Clubman I was travelling in shone its headlights onto a black dog wandering along the side of the road. My mother, who was driving, has an instinctive belief that every life is in peril and in need of someone to save it. The dog, just by being out on the road at night, *needed* to be saved. So she stopped the car and bundled it onto the back seat to sit on top of my brother and me. Now on a mission to find the owner, she drove into Fosdyke, stopping at a pub to ask – in the familiar emotional tone reserved for all personal and national calamities – whether anyone knew whose dog it was. The pub must have been the Ship Inn, which is still there. Of all the animals in the world to rescue, she'd chosen the most undistinguishable: everyone had a black dog, or knew of a black dog, or wondered whether a dark brown dog might be called a black dog in certain lights. My mother has the knack of getting other people involved in her dramas. She stood, not budging an inch. Eventually one of the men gave in, suggesting a house where he thought they might have a dog that might be black.

One thing to note here is that my mother never gives up, anything, and certainly not when she is out to save something. She made him sketch a map and we drove off, along a very small and straight fenland road that vanished into the gloom. Along it was the occasional bungalow, and she eventually stopped at one of them. The rain beat down on the windows of the car. She dragged the dog to the front door and knocked for a long time. I believe her morale must have started to crumble. Certainly when she tells me this story she always says how stupid she was feeling by then. And even more so when, having called through the letterbox several times, she finally tried the handle and found the house was unlocked. She went in, calling out for the owner, but there was no one around. It was the end of her quest. She shoved the dog inside – a muddy black dog that showed neither recognition of, nor unfamiliarity with, the place – leaving a puzzle for someone else to sort out.

That was the way my mother saved things. A few miles further down the road, on the same journey, the car hit a pigeon. She pulled over onto the verge once more, and when she picked the bird off the tarmac she realised – by the way its wing was hanging – that a bone had snapped. She must have thought she was being put through a test, or that her car was attracting these problems towards it. This time, she took the pigeon to a different pub, in Sutterton. She laid it on a bar mat and commanded the men to step forward, to fix its wing, and make it fly again.

She climbed back in the car and stared stoically through the windscreen.

'They're going to put it in a pie,' she said, sadly.

We picked many birds off the road in the '70s, and tried to fix their broken anatomies with sellotape and lollipop sticks. We gave these birds – mostly sparrows and blackbirds – optimistic names like 'Lucky' and 'Hope', and would look after them for several days, keeping them in the living room and feeding them worms we'd dug up in the garden, or bits of cold ham. The birds would watch us suspiciously from the corners of their boxes, and after a few days they would die, with a film of some unknown skin descending across their eye before they lay down and gave up. We'd bury them in the flowerbed, and occasionally our cat Honey would exhume them, making us believe that instead of saving them, we'd actually made them die twice.

You try, you try your best, and sometimes you make things worse.

Near Fosdyke, Heath and I called into a café by the side of the road, where I told him the story of the black dog.

'I'm glad your mother did that,' he replied. 'She may not have solved the mystery, but she was part of the chain of people that did. She played her part, and that's all that any of us can do.'

Heath was in a particularly philosophical mood. He sometimes needs to find meaning in a story, whereas I am the opposite: I think there are many stories that don't have a particular meaning, and don't need to find one. They are just there, to be told.

'Fosdyke is that kind of place,' he added.

'What do you mean?'

'Even the dogs try to get away. This dog you've told me about, it may not have known it, but being out there in the dark on the edge of the village – it sounds in tune with the general sense of unease around here.'

We had this conversation just inside the door, and I was slow to realise that the café was entirely empty. There was no one serving at the counter, and no one sitting at any of the tables, despite several of them having triangular metal *reserved* signs on them. The room smelt of jacket potatoes and bleach. It was eerily quiet, and made me think I'd just wandered into someone's house, like my mother must have felt when she opened the door to that unlocked bungalow all those years ago. Perhaps all the buildings in Fosdyke are deserted, or have the tendency to revert to that state when no one's looking.

A chalkboard above the fireplace had a list of bar snacks. Jacket potatoes with chilli, with bacon bits, with chicken curry, with tuna mayonnaise. The tables had the waxed gloss finish of mass-produced pine furniture that can look like they're made of cheddar cheese.

'I don't like it here,' I whispered to Heath.

'Me neither.'

At the back of the room, the door to the kitchen looked ominous. We left before anyone came to serve us.

'Anyway,' Heath added, back on the pavement, 'in my opinion the jacket potato is a gastronomic crime against such a proud vegetable.'

I fussed with my bike, expecting a lecture on English root vegetables that didn't, in fact, come.

He cycled off, and I thought about that black dog again, and whether the story did in fact have meaning after all. Could the black dog be an emblem of how this strange landscape might be read? Does the black dog represent a disturbance out there, something that is wrong and lost and needs to be put back into a correct place? Or does it have no meaning at all? When you break it all down and try to sort it out, you find yourself setting off on a new journey, where questions are not answered, but are merely followed by more questions.

Fleet Fen

By this point in our journey I thought I'd learnt a few things about the flatness of the Lincolnshire fens. But as we entered the South Holland district, back on the A17, the land looked like it had been scraped down to an even more perfect level, and after so much dark peaty soil, the ground became lighter, sandier, and now had the scorched look of a desert. In New York there'd been that list of hills marked on the bus route, none of them higher than a few feet, but here in South Holland the landscape was so flat my gaze became instantly twitchy, wanting to latch onto anything it could.

A set of fence posts running alongside the road seemed inordinately high and straight. An electricity substation, behind a chain-linked fence, resembled a futuristic cityscape. A concrete water hydrant became an ancient obelisk. In this landscape, an iron sluice gate can seem like a cubist masterpiece hanging over a channel of water and, in spring, squares of bright tulips can transform a field into a dazzling six-acre Mondrian.

I paused in a layby and listened to the area's desert sound. Taking a few steps to the verge, the grit under my shoes made a noise like I was grinding peppercorns. An insect passed by, its wings drilling the air like helicopter rotors. I imagined I'd be able to hear a ladybird crawling up a blade of grass, as it climbed towards the sky's immense volume and stillness. Like any true desert, this area drew me to both the infinite and the immediate, and I was reminded of a time when I'd been walking in Timna Park, in Israel's Negev desert, and in particular how I'd been fascinated there by the view of endless dust and rock in bands of ochre and red and yellow, with the distant mountains of Jordan appearing to float like zeppelins in the heat haze, and being simultaneously aware of the flies around me and the sounds of my sandals on the bare rock. The rock was as hot as a kiln. Flies landed on my arm, my skin glistened with sweat, and in the distance those mountains slid silently into view like a giant set change in a theatre. I was reliving this moment when an agricultural lorry suddenly rushed by with the force of a locomotive, dragging the air around it like a tornado. A carrot flew from the top of its cargo, and landed a few feet away from me on the tarmac. It lay there, stunned, as the silence took over again.

We rode off on our bikes, passing fields of bright green crops. Telegraph poles lent perilously this way and that, as the soil pulled them down. Traffic signs had a crust of dirt on them, made from dust storms of topsoil and the spray of passing lorries. As we cycled by, the geometric rows of cauliflower and cabbage began to flicker like a zoetrope. It made me want to take my eyes off the road and stare at them instead, to become hypnotised by their strobing pattern, expecting the vegetables to perform a simple, endlessly repeating acrobatic circus trick.

I came up with a simple poem to accompany the turning of my pedals:

The potato has eyes
The wheat has ears
And the caulis have their heads.

But only the artichoke
Has a heart.

The ticking back wheel of my bike lulled me into a trance where road, field and sky seemed to collude into a landscape that was full of deceptive qualities. The more I pedalled, the longer the road appeared, while objects in the distance seemed to be sliding away instead of getting closer. I noticed peculiar objects in people's front gardens. One house had the top of a mast sunk in the lawn, with dozens of ceramic insulators nailed to it like a semi-industrial totem pole. A bungalow had a brightly-painted tractor placed at each corner of its garden. There were ornamental windmills and gnomes lurking in the flowerbeds. And this, by the side of the road, a tray selling sharp objects, next to a puzzling sign that read like a maths problem:

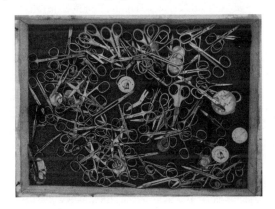

ANY ITEM 50P
THREE ITEMS £1
SEVEN ITEMS £2
ELEVEN ITEMS £3
FIFTEEN ITEMS £4
TWENTY ITEMS £5

Standing in front of the Anglia Motel, across two bays of the car park, was a Hawker Hunter jet plane. By its front wheel was a sign, suggesting a 25p donation if you wanted to take a selfie there. It bothered me that the plane seemed to be straddling the car bays, and that its nose pointed towards a fence fifty feet away. A landed plane deserved a straight line of empty space in front of it, I thought. A runway, or at least a road that could be used as one. Instead, it was wedged into a corner as though a giant child had left it there, giving the impression that in other car parks in Lincolnshire there might be more supersized toys, like colossal Playmobil figures or house-sized blocks of Lego.

A placard told us that this Hawker Hunter first flew on 6th October 1954, and that after only three years in the air, it was assigned for training on the ground. It had some time at the Defence Test and Evaluation Organisation facility at Aberporth, before being moved to its current spot (having been repainted) in 2005. What the sign failed to explain was why a jet plane ever ended up outside a fenland motel, or what sort of reaction it was trying to provoke. To me, it felt unsettling, like seeing a ship washed up on shore, or – in my mother's eyes – a black dog lost in a black night. Each thing has its own place in the world, and needs to be returned there.

From a distance, the Hawker Hunter looked as if it was still up for a bit of war, if called upon. But close up, it looked faded. There was rust on its bays, and weeping stains along its undercarriage. Its wheels were slightly deflated, and I thought of one of my friends who makes intricate models of British warplanes in his flat in Islington. He also grew up in Norfolk, where he was harassed by American fighter jets flying over his house. The model making is a kind of therapy, I suppose. I asked him once if he used sandpaper to flatten the plastic at the base of the wheels, to give the appearance of the plane's weight as it stood. No, he replied, only the amateurs do that. The pros use an iron – touching each wheel to make the plastic flatten but also slightly bulge. Done correctly, tiny plastic wheels can look as though they're full of air. Reality, and its imitation, can blur.

After our failure to eat at Fosdyke – or lack of nerve – we were both hungry. We went into the café at the Anglia Motel – a place my family have always called *The Flags*, because for several years it had a row of flagpoles next to it with the most tattered flags I've ever seen flying in this country. The Union Jack, when I last saw it, had shredded away to a strip of cloth no wider than a bandage, like someone was flying the waistband of a pair of boxers. When I told this to Heath, he thought it was apt that the nation's flag was being slowly undone here. The fens don't really belong to England, he said, not if popularity is a judge of their worth. The nation turns its back on them. In geological terms, too – he added – they're really not part of the country. They are a section of the North Sea's seabed.

As transport cafés go, the Anglia Motel at Fleet Hargate might just deserve a rosette for *Greasy Spoon Best in Show*. Able to seat three or four hundred people, it is vast, with one section having wooden tables and chairs and gingham tablecloths, conjoined to a larger extension where the tables are Formica and the chairs are moulded out of a lurid nectarine-coloured plastic. It feels as though a 1970s Technicolor spaceship crashed into the older café, and you can time travel between the different decades just by stepping across the separating join on the floor. There are trestle tables covered in bric-a-brac, an Artex ceiling that resembles a cave roof and, along the back wall, a row of intimidating fridge cabinets rattle away while, above them, a dazzling display of menus are written out on multi-coloured Day-Glo card, like a hallucinogenic haze.

Heath stood there as if he'd been struck. 'Wow,' he said. It's a word he doesn't usually use.

'Look over there,' I whispered. We shuffled over to the first of the refrigerated cabinets where we encountered the biggest custard tarts I've ever seen – each one the size of a kid's beach bucket. Further back in the cabinet were slabs of bread pudding like inflatable mattresses, covered with pale margarine as thick as a tongue. Heath and I stared at them for quite some time.

'I dare you,' I muttered.

'No,' he replied, 'they could kill you, on the spot.'

While Heath ate a bean burger and I ate scampi and chips, I asked him why he'd called his dog Half-Shandy. His explanation was that he'd been drinking in the *Champion of the Thames* pub on King Street in Cambridge when someone came in with a new-born litter of whippet puppies: 'He handed them round to anyone who wanted one. There were five puppies, and they naturally all got named after drinks behind the bar. There was a Whiskey, a Kahlua, a Curacao and a Jägermeister, though I think that one was renamed Tiny when they got him home. I took to this little one here, with his shandy-coloured coat, and because he really could have fitted in a half-pint glass.'

Half-Shandy sat beneath the table, curled round Heath's legs, aware that he was being talked about. The dog had fascinated me all day – after trotting nervously down the Langrick Road, he'd quickly given up to take a ride in Heath's basket, then later on he'd been bounding at full pelt along the Fleet Fen road. The dog seemed to have two primary gears: first gear – sleep, and second gear – mad-dash hurtle where he became blurred.

'Here, pick a card,' Heath said, producing a deck from his inside pocket. He has many surprising things in his pockets. He fanned them out in his hand.

'You've shown me this one,' I said. 'It's the one where my card becomes the only one facing out.'

'Oh – have I? In that case, a new one, pick two cards.'

I went along with the trick, picking a couple of cards and watching Heath as he did various shuffling manoeuvres and sleights of hand. He's actually quite good, though he seemed to find this trick awkward.

'I think I may have gone wrong somewhere,' he muttered, looking puzzled. I wondered whether this was part of his showman-patter, but no, he really had gone wrong. He only guessed one of my two cards correctly.

I sat back in my chair and wondered about what we looked like: Heath examining the cards with a sense they'd let him down, an unfinished bean burger on his plate, and me with a map and camera on the table while Half-Shandy looked up expectantly from below, surrounded by a café that was overdosed with gaudy neon coloured menus and supersized bottles of ketchup and brown sauce.

I should have known that the usual principals of size and relativity didn't really apply here – especially with those bread puddings that could flatten you – because in the corridor on the way to the toilet I stopped in my tracks to stare in wonder at the Artex ceiling above me. It wasn't the Artex itself that was so fascinating, but rather the fluorescent tube stuck onto it. As I stared up at the ceiling the plaster on either side of the light began to bend like the pages of an open book, and in the gap where the light was I thought I saw a glimpse through a wormhole of time into an alternative universe.

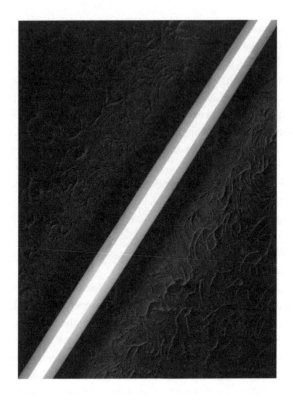

It was like my moment standing on the gravestones inside Boston Stump, where time briefly had a depth, rather than a direction.

In a side room I came across a homemade display about the Normandy landings and the Royal British Legion. An elderly man was sitting by the display in a serviceman's jacket and beret, and on the other side a woman who might have been his wife was having a cup of tea. In the softly flattened vowels of the fenland accent, the man told me he'd been on Gold Beach as part of the landings, and had fought his way across Europe to Hamburg, but had missed VE day by two days because he was on leave at the time.

I asked him about the jet plane in the car park outside. He looked out through the doorway, almost to check it was still there. 'She used to be tilted back, with her nose sticking up like this,' he said, angling his old hand up for me. 'It looked like she was going to take off.' He smiled happily. We looked at the plane outside which, back on all its wheels, looked more like a car.

'Tell you a secret,' he added. 'She's painted all wrong. As a Mk.1 she wouldn't have worn them colours in service.'

The motel, above the café, was our place for the night. I was shown a room I guessed was usually inhabited by farm labourers, hauliers, and the occasional travelling salesman. It had a simple single bed and a floral duvet, and a print of a poppy hanging on the wall. I looked at the window and briefly imagined old Miss Claypole's eyes sliding down the glass, which I tried to dispel because an image like that doesn't help in a place like this. Outside, I could see the car park, the corner of an agricultural supplier's yard, and a ploughed field beyond. The light was already going, and the relentless rush of farming lorries on the A17 was beginning to calm down. I heard starlings filling a tree with their strange evening murmurs, as though the animal life that had been absent from the desert flatland all day was only now emerging, to come home. It had been a strange and long day, beginning in New York, working its way through Boston and across Holland Fen to Fosdyke and Fleet. I felt confused by it – by a sense of collecting fragments along the way. A notebook filling up with observations, a camera loaded up with pictures, and a daunting sense of a landscape which would at some point have to be corralled and shaped into some sense of meaning. Would the journey ever make sense to me? I wondered. The fens felt large, the journey felt large, and I seemed to be just scratching at the surface, worrying away at some particular aspect, while there was a real chance I would never find what I was searching for. I looked at some of the photos I'd taken: a doorway in New York of the house named Brooklyn, a picture of a crossroads, photos of the bread puddings and custard tarts in the café below. There was a connection to be made between them, and simultaneously, no connection at all.

I woke in the middle of the night and wondered where I was. When I recognised my motel room, I felt only partially reassured. Where I was still seemed a valid question. Through the window I saw the Hawker Hunter in the car park. I imagined the refrigerated cabinets in the café beneath me, with the world's largest bread puddings left in a pile in the dark, lit by the pale blue glow of an electric flytrap. Custard tarts, slightly sweating, waiting to be eaten. I shuddered to think I'd be back down there soon, for a breakfast that would bully me. The first light of dawn was already in the sky. Occasional lorries passed by on the A17, their cabs lit up like Christmas trees, taking asparagus and artichokes and potatoes to the nation, and I thought about a photo I had of my grandfather's wellington boots, with 'walking in the daffs,' as he described it, on the back. The photo was taken only a mile away from where I was, in Fleet Fen, but over half a century ago, and I wondered how he'd felt out there, walking the rows of sprouting bulbs, while his boots collected mud until it was several inches thick and it must have seemed he could go no further, that he was turning into mud himself, that he would always be stuck in this place.

Tilting at Wind Farms

The next morning was breezy and the air smelt fresh with salt. We went downstairs to the café, where we both settled for poached eggs on brown toast with a side of fried tomatoes. Above the counter the Day-Glo menus shone down at us, like they had the day before, but now we felt desensitised to them. The café seemed full of morning optimism. A radio was playing from inside the kitchen, and all things seemed possible.

We had just finished breakfast when Heath ambushed me with a plan: 'Let's cycle over to see the Gedney wind farm,' he said. 'You know, there are six turbines, built in 2006. Each one has an eighty-two-metre rotor diameter.'

I watched him align his knife and fork precisely on his plate, wondering how he knew these kind of facts. Perhaps he'd picked up a leaflet somewhere, or had spent the night surfing the Net on his old phone although, really, the Internet is not necessary to a man like Heath – what he doesn't know, he's quite happy to make up.

We'd seen the wind turbines the day before, presiding over the fen a few miles away. Out there even a telephone pole looked tall, so the giant masts and rotor blades were impossible to ignore. But after breakfast, when we set off on the lane to Gedney, they proved surprisingly hard to reach. The road kept turning at corners of fields, and the wind farm – just there in front of us – was suddenly over there at a right angle, then it would vanish, then reappear again this time over our shoulders. How could something so large and dominant, and in such a flat landscape, disappear so easily? It was like a great conjuring trick.

Eventually we found a sign placed into a hedge, announcing: *Gedney Wind Farm E30 and E31*. From beyond the hawthorn we could hear the relentless shrieking of the rotor blades, which was a deeply unsettling sound. We entered the field and saw all six turbines spinning fast. Each blade was the length and colour of a passenger aircraft's wing, but with a carving knife's narrowness that looked unhinged and dangerous. We approached the first turbine. The blades whipped through the air with a pulsing howl, and although the hub of the turbine must have been five-storeys high, the tips of gleaming white steel slashed above our heads at a distance that was difficult to gauge. The sensation that this curve of gleaming white steel was about to cut us into a grave was overwhelming. Perhaps perhaps it's the fact that wind turbines tend to have three blades that makes them particularly disturbing: they revolve with an asymmetry that feels uncontrolled. Four blades might have more balance, and five or six would make them spin like a wheel. But three feels deranged.

We instinctively crouched beneath the turbine. The ferocious chopping of the air above us made it feel like the sky was being rearranged, divided and constantly reordered. Nothing could settle. In the field next to us, the shadow of the blades swept across the crowns of cauliflowers with a neurotically fast whip. I pictured the caulis as rows of men buried up to their necks in the soil, trying to pull leafy hands over their heads. Late in the day, this shadow must cover the entire field – it would be an alarming sight: a crow's wing of fear scything across the veg. I couldn't help thinking the cauliflowers would be affected, that they'd grow under this shadow with a bitter taste.

I told Heath that wind turbines kill thousands of birds each year. Building them here, in the flight path of migration routes must be disastrous. 'Take the swans coming in to Welney,' I said, 'they've flown several thousand miles from Siberia, they've crossed the tundra, then Scandinavia, they've flown over the North Sea and the Wash and, finally, within sight of those breeding grounds at Welney, they have to chance their luck through a field of flying daggers.'

'You're being sentimental,' he replied. 'And inaccurate. There's no proof of that.'

I began to look for bodies of birds around the base of the turbine. A dead swan would be a persuasive argument. As I moved behind the mast the sound of the wind changed. It became quieter, whooshing with vortex. There were no dead birds.

Heath followed me, inspecting the bolts that fixed the steel mast to a massive cement plinth. I noticed a perfect string of footprints where a bird had wandered round the base just after the cement was poured, and pointed them out to Heath.

He shrugged: 'That was merely a curious bird. It came to no harm.'

But I was having none of it: 'Or that bird pitched into the Wash with its new pair of concrete boots.'

I thought of the bird, flapping heavily towards the sea, its feet set in concrete, and immediately thought of my grandfather's boots, inch thick with mud, in the photo taken at Fleet Fen. Touch the ground in this area, and you become rooted, dangerously so.

Gedney Drove End

The visit to the wind farm played in my favour, because just along the road –
among various local signs for Gedney Dyke, Gedney Dawsmere, Gedney Hill
and Gedney Broadgate – was the one to Gedney Drove End.

Gedney Drove End has an almost mythical significance for my family
because it's here that my mother, as a newly qualified teacher, drove for
an interview in 1977. After a long journey that must have made her believe
she was returning to parts of a fenland childhood she'd hoped to leave
behind, she arrived here, at a sparse and half-deserted village wedged
between cabbage fields, marshes and an RAF bombing range. She sat in
her car, dressed in her interview suit with her hair tied up, outside the
small primary school, and decided no, there's no way she was even going
to give it a chance. She turned the ignition key and drove the sixty miles
back home.

I've often pictured my mum at that moment, reaching the crux of a
decision, with two sons back in Norwich not knowing how close they might
be to a new life, living on the edge of nowhere in the Lincolnshire fen. The
moment feels precious and fragile, as though she was mentally standing a
coin on the car's dashboard, with two alternative lives exerting pressure
on both sides. I wonder what was the precise moment of decision – was
it the sight of the school door, painted a colour that seemed poignant and
hopeless? Or was it something more unpredictable she didn't like – the
sight of a man out walking his dog, say, giving it an extra, unnecessary tug
on the lead? Something tipped her, and my life in Gedney Drove End never
happened.

But it was a close call. There was a house among these houses that would have become the family home. The people Heath and I passed on our bikes: in a parallel universe, these people were my friends.

Gedney Drove End didn't really have a centre, and just beyond the village the buildings petered out and the road stopped being a road, becoming a track across a single field instead. It came to an end at a space just wide enough to turn a car, in front of an imposing flood bank.

We left the bikes and climbed the bank, where we had a glorious sight of saltmarshes, beyond which there was a thick band of mud and only then, in the thinnest of strips, the open sea of The Wash. We'd been travelling alongside the sea since a few miles out of Boston, the previous day, but only now had it finally come into sight. In the far distance, across the Wash, we could see the cliffs at Hunstanton. It was our first glimpse of Norfolk, fifteen miles away, and it appeared like a mirage. Those cliffs were the first elevated piece of landscape we'd seen since New York.

'I remember this place,' I said to Heath, struck by a sudden memory of a sunny evening in the late '70s. 'My mother brought me and my brother near here – and she drove up to a car park and when she stopped she said "right – who wants to roll about in mud?" It's funny – I haven't thought about it for years. But we were out of that car like a shot, stripping off into our underwear, running into one of the mud creeks. She stood on the bank laughing at us, telling us to "Roll about, do somersaults, do what you like!"'

'And did you?'

'Of course we did. We got drunk out there, tumbling about in it, wrestling, sliding, cutting our feet on all these buried shells in the mud.'

I remembered how all three of us had eventually reached the sea, where we washed off as best as we could in the freezing water. It's a moment that sums up the freedom I felt in my childhood, boundless in every direction, and from where I was now standing on the flood bank I thought fondly about those three figures, out there on the saltmarsh, having the time of their lives, so tiny in such a vast landscape.

The Wash itself is a dynamic part of the North Sea, swirling with shifting sandbanks and racing tidal currents, eating into the eastern side of the country like a giant bite. It's over two hundred square miles of water, but is very hard to actually reach: marshes, creeks, tidal flats and sand bars get in the way – making the coast an oddly absent phenomenon in this part of England. The other obstacle here at Gedney is the RAF Holbeach bombing range, which stretches for several miles along the marsh. From the top of the flood bank we could see a series of utilitarian control towers built along the footpath, and set into the saltmarsh below them were a pattern of targets, flags and small manmade hills with range-finding markers round their bases. A little further out, old hulks of rusted boats had been painted orange and white to simulate convoys and ships ready to be bombed or strafed.

A woman was walking along the flood bank with an elderly Labrador on an extendable lead. Half-Shandy greeted it, and both dogs touched noses, wagging their tails in friendship. The woman waited patiently for the dogs to have their meeting, and noticed Heath was watching the wind turbines beyond the village.

'The year they were built,' she said, 'twenty-nine windows were smashed in the church, and then the altar cloth was set on fire.'

'Do you think those two things are connected?' I asked.

She shrugged, then looked at the marsh with a dreamy gaze. Gedney must breed this kind of expression. If my mum had taken that job at the school, I would probably know things about this woman: I might know that her husband was an agricultural mechanic in Spalding, that she was saving up to go on a Baltic cruise one day, that her garden was known for spring peonies, that she once put a plaster on my knee when I fell off a bike, that her daughter was at the school with me but was now at technical college in Peterborough, that she worked in a café until she had a health scare which made her go part time, where she could spend more of her days out here walking her dog. I would know the dog's name.

'What's your dog called?' I asked.

'Poppy.'

'Nice to meet you, Poppy,' I said, patting the dog.

Heath and I walked up to one of the RAF control towers, which was deserted but covered with various notices about trespassing and its consequences. Loudspeakers stuck out from the corners of the building like bracket fungi. Below us, a sign standing in the marsh had a picture of a bomb exploding, alongside a particularly stark warning:

DO NOT TOUCH ANY MILITARY DEBRIS.
IT MAY EXPLODE AND KILL YOU.

Heath and I are both paid up members of CND, but these military zones fascinate us. I blame the fact that I was brought up when Norfolk was a de-facto landing strip for the RAF and the USAF, flying their supersonic playthings and, occasionally, shaking my bedroom window nearly out of the frame when they broke the sound barrier. As a result my childhood was – like like that of every child growing up in East Anglia – unhealthily dominated by thoughts of nuclear war. At primary school the US Air Force F-111 strategic bombers and Thunderbolt A-10 Warthogs roared over the playground, tearing the sky apart with their jet-shrieks several times a day, endlessly practising war games. The airfields of Lakenheath, Coltishall, Mildenhall and Rendlesham were bristling with planes, and the presence of all this military hardware was clearly making us a target for the snub-nosed Soviet SS20s that were crawling through the forests of Russia on the backs of camouflaged lorries, ready for launching. The joke went that if ever you were lost in Norfolk, phone the Kremlin, because they knew the county backwards, and would be able to direct you if you were, say, at the Matlaske crossroads trying to get to the Saracen's Head. I would go to sleep at night thinking of East Anglian maps laid out on dark wooden tables in austere

Kremlin war rooms, of military generals shouting orders down old Bakelite phones, mispronouncing *Colt-tish-hall* or *Mun –des –lee*, and then in the cruel montage of my dream, I'd imagine that crude Soviet rocketry hurtling its way across the North Sea, on its six minute journey towards my bedroom. And when you grew up on the coast, you fully expected to see, one day, those rockets passing over the cliff tops, a few seconds before the flash.

Gedney was an incredibly peaceful place, in the same way that the end of the road always seems to be a peaceful place, where journeys peter out and all you can do is pause. It was peculiar to imagine Tornadoes, Harriers and Jaguars screeching across this marsh, sending down hellfire missiles to blow up plywood targets and plastic barrels among the marram and samphire. Occasionally, American B2 bombers fly a round trip of twenty hours, from their bases in the United States, to drop bombs on Gedney from 23,000 feet, before heading back home without ever landing. It seems a thoroughly odd exercise to go to all that trouble just to bomb a part of English saltmarsh. Americans bombing England, and no one mentioning it. Between each bombing raid, the saltmarsh here would have the same hum of sunlight and gentle buzz of insects and bees that all saltmarshes have. Sanderlings would run along the creek beds, crabs would blow bubbles from their mouths, skylarks would return to the sky. The same airy breeze would settle and stir the grasses.

What do the pilots think, I wondered, as they approached these targets at several hundred miles an hour? Do they try and forget the marsh, imagining the deserts and wadis of the Middle East instead, or do they think nothing at all – that it's all in a day's work to bomb a part of Lincolnshire? I realised the blasts have become a part of this landscape, just as the Plain of Jars in Laos, the island of Malta, or the Nevada Test Site have irrevocably changed since being labelled the most bombed places on Earth. You can't just keep bombing a place and expect the land itself to remain unaffected. There are various target hills on US military bases that have been fired at for so many years they now glitter with shrapnel and unexploded ordinance, and will possibly never again be safe to set foot on. Their landscape has evolved into a new category, where danger and proximity to death have become part of the way we understand them. And it is ironic that extreme military use actually turns some of these areas into wilderness again, free from man, like the anthrax island of Gruinard, in the Scottish Highlands, or the pacific atolls of Bikini and Enewetak that were eviscerated by atomic weapons, and where the only sound now is the peaceful lapping of waves. And I thought some of this quality existed out there on the Gedney Marsh, where the relentless bombing and strongly worded keep out signs had actually made a kind of forbidden sanctuary for nature to thrive in.

Think, Don't Sink!

Oh well, let them bomb Gedney, I thought, as we cycled off. No one will notice. We followed the ruler-straight line of the River Nene, which lay fat as a motorway between thick banks of mud, to Sutton Bridge. In the trips we used to take to Boston in my mother's white Mini Clubman, Sutton Bridge was a notorious place because, in April 1979, during the period when we used to take this road every other weekend, a man had been shot in a hold-up on the petrol forecourt here. In the months after the murder, that pale glass kiosk between the petrol pumps took on the aspect of a display case, keeping what had happened inside it very much in our minds. My brother and I would whisper to each other in the back seat, describing blood splattering the glass, trying to freak each other out, and coming up with various scenarios of who the killer might have been, where they'd vanished to, and who the unlucky bugger was who'd had to wipe that blood off with a sponge after the police had finished gathering evidence.

We never filled up with petrol there.

A new attendant, of course, was soon employed, and he sat in the same glass box where the previous man had been murdered, with an inscrutable attitude. A man who looks bored to the bone can also easily look like a dead man. Perhaps he was never told about his predecessor. But to us it was clear: that man sat under a sword of Damocles.

In accordance with the principle that all things will vanish, or manage to reinvent themselves, that kiosk was eventually dismantled, the concrete forecourt broken up and the fuel tanks dug out. Later, new foundations were built, walls erected and a roof fitted, and double-glazed windows were inserted to block out the noise of the A17. A new room was furnished with thick carpet and lined with shelves. A television, placed in the corner, figurines and children's photos put in frames on an ornamental mantelpiece – precisely in the spot where the attendant's last moments had been lived, his miscalculated scuffle to protect the money that was never his own, the killer's finger pressing the cold edge of the shotgun's trigger, the sudden splatter of blood, surprisingly bright, and the moment that could never be retreated from – it all happened in a space which has now vanished entirely. The murder, removed. And as we cycled up to the place where all this had happened, I wanted to knock on one of those house doors and ask them whether they have felt anything odd about the end of the sofa where they sit to watch TV, because it's exactly the place where a man was once shot to death.

The murdered man, Gordon Snowden, has the briefest of mentions on the Internet, because his life and death belong to an age before the worldwide web, and no one is interested now in solving the murder of a pump attendant which happened nearly forty years ago. His murderer has no mention, because they were never caught. If a search is made for 'murder in Sutton Bridge' there is instead far more chatter about a more recent killing in nearby Long Sutton, in November 2008. And in the way the Internet has of answering one search with a different answer – much like an elderly aunt who cannot keep to the subject – I turned my attention to this murder as a way of understanding the unresolved one from my youth. It started when a woman moved a large plasma TV into her bedroom so that she could spend her nights playing *Grand Theft Auto*. Her ten-year-old son would play GTA until midnight, and then she would take over, riding the streets of Los Santos or Liberty City until 5am, shooting up and driving by, unaware that her husband was feeling more and more marginalised downstairs. Bottling it up, he'd taken to sleeping on a sofa in the conservatory. The inevitable violence – which anyone other than those involved might have seen coming – finally erupted during a blazing row, not conducted on the pixelated sidewalks of San Andreas, but in the disappointingly mundane environment of the couple's own bedroom in Long Sutton, where after fetching two knives from the kitchen drawer he stabbed her thirty times, in front of the screen where *Grand Theft Auto* depicted a world of violence and no escape. The murder was overheard by their son, who phoned 999, and while the operator was still taking down the details, the murdering husband and father came to the phone with the words: 'I'm sorry. I think I've killed her,' in a voice that could have come from the soundtrack of the game itself.

We paused on the old iron swing bridge, looking down at the River Nene, which led to the sea in a relentlessly straight line. The water smelt of seaweed and brine. Heath asked 'where next?' in a tone that suggested he had a plan I might not like.

'I thought we'd search for King John's treasure.'

'Many have looked.'

Across the river was a large area of fen that used to be known as Walpole Island, where King John supposedly lost his entire baggage train containing the crown jewels in 1216, the year after he signed Magna Carta. It's recorded that the king had had chronic indigestion that day, from eating too many lampreys in Wisbech Castle, and could do nothing while the quicksand swallowed up his gold. Over the centuries there have been repeated attempts to find the treasure, and it's still a common sight to see someone with a metal detector out there. But so far the fenland soil has been reluctant to give up its hoard.

'I think all we might manage to dig up are cabbages,' Heath said.

'I take it you have an alternative up your sleeve?'

'How about we go to Pinchbeck?'

'Why?' I asked.

'The Key Market Store was the first place in the country to scan a barcode, in 1979. I read about it. The barcode was printed on a packet of Melrose teabags.'

'You want to go there?'

'Not really – it's a Morrisons supermarket, now. But I do have another idea. It's so flat here the cycling is easy. I thought we could detour to Welney. We can follow the path of your migrating swans – the ones that got through the blades of the wind turbines, that is.'

'That's – twenty miles away. It's not really en route to California.'

'What *is* en route?' he replied, suggesting that a far larger issue of what constitutes a route between two places needed to be addressed. 'It's unanswerable.'

I knew I wasn't going to win this one.

'What's at Welney?' I asked.

'You'll see.'

'I'd rather you tell me.'

'OK. At Welney we will find ourselves on a different planet. One that doesn't obey the ordinary rules of physics. Does that answer your question?'

My migratory sense told me it was the wrong way, but I suppose I was intrigued, because we decided to leave King John's famous treasure somewhere in the fenland mud, and set off for Welney. Heath was being annoyingly enigmatic, but I let it pass. He usually manages to unearth the not quite visible, I reminded myself.

The route took us through the villages of Walpole St Peter and Marshland St James, where we stuck to the tiny droves that wound their way through the fen. On either side of the tarmac, the fields were either black with richly ploughed soil, or vivid green with the fresh leaves of tightly packed rows of beet, cabbage and potato. We cycled through clouds of air pungent with the lingering smell of brassicas, then the stale fishy smell of rapeseed, the sharp scent of onions and the graveyard stink of bone meal. Across the fields, lines of poplars dissected the view as windbreaks, and electricity pylons stretched to the horizon, underlining a rigid geometry stronger in this landscape than in any other part of Britain. Fields were laid out with precision, filled with the cross hatching of vegetable rows.

This picture, from my grandfather's collection, sums up the sometimes baffling nature of the fenland landscape. The horse appears to have no owner, and seems hell-bent on doing the levelling job all by itself. Its face seems ghostly, and to the right of the horse there seems to be a spectral smudge in the shape of a man. The furrows make little sense, and the line of seed in the soil looks almost like it's just been uncovered as the horse reverses, like an impossible streak of quartz where there is no rock.

As we cycled, I remembered that it was somewhere around here that I once won a turkey. I have a recollection of standing in a draughty room and pointing at a large white bird through the wintry glass of an old farmhouse window, but it's possible I'm confusing that place with another: a turkey farm in North Norfolk where you choose your bird as it pecks about the yard, then, a few weeks later, return for the fattened body and, before you pick it up, are forced to walk through a room ankle deep in the plucked white feathers of countless slaughtered others. In the centre of the room, as symbolically placed as an altar, is a waist-high chopping block, where all the killing was done, with a couple of long knives left on the wood.

I have no reliable memory of how I won that fenland turkey. But I remember fragments of the journey I took to pick the bird up. It had been before the age of sat nav, and a series of signposts I came to managed to point towards the same village names, but in different orders and multiple directions at every junction. Each crossroad, four villages pointed to, then at the next crossroad, four more, on signposts where it looked highly possible that – given a little effort (if you were feeling mischievous) – you could spin the names around. During World War II these signposts would have been taken down altogether, to confuse and thwart any invasion from the Wash. And as I drove round in circles and squares, all I could think about were phantom columns of German infantry – heavy equipment, supplies and artillery, the whole machinery of an invading army – also going round in circles and squares in this relentlessly featureless landscape, scratching heads at each corner, growing ever more dispirited and, ultimately, defeated before a single shot was fired. It happened before, when the Roman military machine came to grief in this same part of the fens, chasing the Anglian tribes hiding out in the infuriating maze of reeds and islands.

Along the road were several signs with the warning:

THINK, DON'T SINK!

On some, there was an image of a car tipping off the road and vanishing into a marsh or river. Clearly the land in this area was still mostly water, or would revert to water without constant drainage, but I couldn't help wondering whether THINK, DON'T SINK! might also be a mental health warning, that thinking your way out of this landscape might be the only way to escape it.

By the side of the road, this car had been abandoned and set on fire. Heath stopped to look at it for a long time. The car still smelt of burnt upholstery and rubber, and the earth around it bore the scorch marks of the blaze. He asked me to take this picture and said: 'You see the face on the underside of the bonnet? It has a skull's eyes, and a despairing mouth.'

Later, I compared it to a photo taken by my grandfather, of his own car – a Humber 9 saloon – taken on 21st November 1929, in this same part of the fens.

My grandfather has been a fleeting presence in this book, and here, I think I see his reflection in the windscreen. Unlike the photo of the abandoned car Heath asked me to take, this car's expression seems friendly, and a little mole-like.

Photographing your car in an unfamiliar environment seems to say a lot about our attitude to landscape itself, and how we need to frame ourselves in it, too. It's not enough to take a picture of the Grand Canyon; you have to place yourself against it, as I once did, standing on the South Rim with my camera propped against a tree. You set the camera's self-timer, rush into position and experience that micro-slice of life which is the camera counting down from eight to zero before the shutter fires. If you were to sum up the human experience, perhaps this eight seconds of waiting has it all: the desire to put yourself in a landscape, to record it for yourself and anyone you know and every future generation, to momentarily put a stop to time, to say YOU WERE THERE on THAT DAY. Perhaps all these things flash through your mind as those eight seconds count down. You choose an expression that shows you off as attractive and capable and LIVING THE DREAM! and hides every doubt you might also have at that one moment. Showing off, yet concealing, all in those eight seconds, like a rodeo rider trying to stay on the bull until the bell rings.

At times like this, I often think of Werner Herzog's droll Germanic narration on his documentaries, where he seems to pull together all manner of observations and comments to shine a light on the human existence. So I might defer to Werner now, sliding over to him the photo of my grandfather's car, and ask him to complete my thoughts here:

Werner: (on voice-over) It was when I saw the photograph of the old car parked by the side of the Lincolnshire dyke that I understood I was seeing the origin of a phenomenon that has gripped the world – of the selfie, the profile shot on social media, the need to demonstrate that all is good, that you are living your life in an attractive and positive manner, and it doesn't matter to you that you have instantly deleted the twenty other digital photos where your mouth was wrong, your hair not right, your expression not quite like the celebrities you admire, and that you have done it all because you crave a *like* or a *thumbs up* or a *bouncing heart-shaped emoji*. You will send it out into the electronic heaven that surrounds us, where it might be glimpsed on a rapidly passing conveyor belt of images as it pings into someone else's day, and all this is fine because everyone else is doing it too, and we're rolling towards a moment where this electronic sarcophagus will dazzle us, celestially lighting up the sky with unreal positivity at the moment when the world ends."

Werner goes on a bit, but you get the point.

A second image of my grandfather's Humber, in 1929, with *The Road* written in his glorious handwriting on the back. It seems he had considerable trouble that day.

We pressed on, wondering whether we, too, would flounder in the fens.

Among the almost volcanic black of the soil, there were sudden pockets of fields filled with brilliant colour. We passed an iris farm, then a rose farm, where the rows of earth were filled with astonishing Technicolor flowers. In the corner of one field, a man was asleep in a parked car. Beyond him was a plot packed with roses in bloom, and I suppose he was there to keep an eye on them. Earlier in the year this area would have been full of rows and rows of tulips, like those in this photo taken by my grandfather near Spalding in 1929:

On both sides of the road, the fields were criss-crossed with a lattice of drainage channels, dykes and rivers. In the fens, nearly all the original rivers have been straightened, some according to Cornelius Vermuyden's grand plan in the 1650s – and others that are still being dredged and managed today with a complicated series of sluice gates, pumping stations and flood defences. It's an elaborate and baffling network, designed to prevent the fens returning to marsh and seawater. Not much of it makes sense. A river flows downhill till it reaches the sea. It's a fairly simple rule. But here – on land as flat as a griddle plate – that rule doesn't always apply. At one point you can be cycling along a riverbank with a channel of water below you when, coming at an oblique angle, a higher bank dissects the landscape, containing a river twenty feet raised in the air. It's like a giant Escher illustration come to life. Some watercourses are flowing, others seem as still as mill ponds covered in rafts of duckweed and water lilies, as if they've not flowed for centuries. Sudden outpourings can surge from sluice gates, pumped from stations miles off in the fields, and channels of water as wide as six-lane motorways can suddenly come to a halt at a dead end. Cumulatively, this water management system is a reminder that alongside, beneath, and sometimes at a height above, a battle is being fought, that this land was once the seabed, or at best a briny marsh, and that the land you are on has merely been borrowed. Viewed this way, the waterways resemble long incisions in the skin of the land, where the fens part to reveal the essential element beneath. Sometimes that water is saline, sometimes it's fresh, depending on how deep the cut.

We pressed on, going deeper into the heartland of the Lincolnshire fens, on ever-smaller roads, into areas where the local dialect is said to have evolved from generations having to speak through gritted teeth, due to the persistence of the cold wind tearing across a landscape that has no obstructions. *Here, there are tigers* could be written on the map – because the people here have a history of rebellion, particularly against the Dutch engineers who first tried to drain the swamp, and still proudly call themselves Fen Tigers when called upon. The vans speeding past us were from freight depots, dog breeders, greenhouse suppliers, plant hire companies and towage companies. And as we continued, I noticed a series of handmade signs along the roadside that, when read together, began to take on the form of a simple haiku:

Asparagus for sale.
Hand-car-washing.
Free manure!
Hard Core wanted.

Yes. It's a hard-core place, I thought.

Four Gotes, Three Holes

It is odd for me to write this chapter heading, because it was also used in my first novel, *Salt*, and putting it here has given me the feeling that my writing has come full circle. On our way to Welney, Heath and I cycled near the strangely named *Four Gotes*, where there was a chicken farm in my novel, and half-an-hour later we arrived at the even-more-strangely named *Three Holes*. The name seems mysterious and inexplicable; that is, until you lean your bike against the railings of the river bridge where – beneath you – three huge drainage channels meet. There, you understand the name very well. Each channel ploughs off to the horizon, where the water eventually blurs into the same element as the sky, in three separate slots, and there appear to be three distinct holes in the view, where land has never completely made a join.

With views like these, it deserves to be a place of pilgrimage, as a place where the land appears to float in triangular sections, like segments of fabric that have nearly been brought together, but not quite hemmed. Heath leant his bike against the railings and looked in admiration along the channels.

'Am I correct in believing some of your first novel is based here?'

I gave him an acknowledging smile. It's quite rare of Heath to admit he's read anything I've written.

'It's where Elsie's family lived in the novel.'

'That's right. The house surrounded by tulips. Where?'

'Down that bank, a few hundred yards.'

'Should we see the house, while we're passing through?'

'There's no house,' I laughed. 'It's all set here, but the house is made up.'

The three channels of water were beginning to make me feel uneasy. They took me to three points on the horizon, like huge arrows, but simultaneously made me feel stuck in their centre, a little like an insect mounted on a pin. It felt as though there was a push and a pull in this part of the landscape, towards distance, but also towards staying put. And from where I was standing, there was no obvious path to where I wanted to go. Our journey should have been following a relatively straight line from New York to California, but so far it had mostly been tangents and detours. Heath had led me on this particular diversion, which had inadvertently brought me to a place I'd once written about. He seemed, in that moment, to be full of mischievous intent, making me revisit past creative ambitions.

Looking at the *Three Holes*, I felt so lost, that I was reminded of Marlowe's despair in *Heart of Darkness*, where 'instead of going to the centre of a continent,' he was 'about to set off for the centre of the Earth.' California, at that point, seemed unreachable.

Fighting for a Flat Earth

In the drainage dyke between Welches dam and Welney bridges, the water was dusted with pollen, and like a single blade of steel it stretched to the horizon, shining with a vertiginous reflection of the sky. For a moment, you might believe a thin slice of air and cloud had been trimmed with scissors, and laid across the ground.

Heath told me why he'd led me on this long detour to Welney. This was the spot where, in 1838, a man called Samuel Birley Rowbottom gazed down the same six-mile length of ruler-straight water and was so fundamentally affected by it that he decided to investigate more thoroughly what he thought he saw. If the Earth was indeed round, it could be proved here with a simple experiment: travelling down this drainage channel, a man standing on a boat should disappear from view – after a distance of just a few miles – because he would vanish beyond the curve of the planet. If the Earth was flat, the man and his rowing boat would stay visible until he eventually went too far to be seen.

Heath described the famous experiment, in which Rowbottom sent his man off in a boat, and waited for him to disappear. A mile passed, then a second, and still he could see the man toiling away at the oars. Then a third, fourth and, finally, five miles, and still – in the rippling optics of extreme distance – he saw the man raise his oar to tap it against the arch of Welney bridge, and it was seen so clearly that Rowbottom must have almost heard the knock of the wood against the brick.

'So it was proved,' I said. 'The Earth was flat after all.'

'Precisely. It made no sense.'

During the writing of this book I found Rowbottom's own description of the experiment, laid out in a rather weighty tome entitled *Zetetic Astronomy*, published in 1881. This is his passage about Welney that day:

> A boat, with a flagstaff, the top of the flag five feet above the surface of the water, was directed to sail from a place called "Welche's Dam" (a well-known ferry passage), to another called "Welney Bridge." These two points are six statute miles apart. The author, with a good telescope, went into the water; and with the eye about eight inches above the surface, observed the receding boat during the whole period required to sail to Welney Bridge. *The flag and the boat were distinctly visible throughout the whole distance!* There could be no mistake as to the distance passed over, as the man in charge of the boat had instructions to lift one of his oars to the top of the arch the moment he reached the bridge. The experiment commenced about three o'clock in the afternoon of a summer's day, and the sun was shining brightly and nearly behind or against the boat during the whole of its passage.

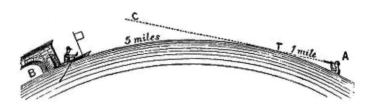

Lurking beyond the outer range of his optics, he thought he spotted barges and wharfs in a murky distance. As a result of this experiment, he began two decades of lecturing around the nation and – because by all accounts he was a formidable debater – the now famous Flat Earth Society was formed.

His experiment is persuasive, although it happily ignores atmospheric conditions and the refractive qualities of light close to warm water. And his book proposing a flat Earth goes on to ignore many other issues, such as – if the Earth is flat – where the sun goes each night, why the moon has phases, why gravity works on Earth but not the stars, why the Southern Hemisphere has winter while we have summer, why your shadow grows longer at a higher latitude, or why his map of the world ended up having a squashed Africa thousands of miles further away from an equally squashed Australia than any maritime journey had ever recorded. Sailing ships would have to zoom like speedboats for it all to make sense. He dismissed these objections as mere trifles, and – as is the way with blind belief – encouraged a vehement following. In 1870 one such man, John Hampden, became so evangelicalistic about the Earth's true flatness, that he made a £500 wager that – at Welney – the theory couldn't be disproved.

Victorian gentlemen liked nothing more than settling a bet, and this particular gambling bait was taken on by the famous naturalist, Alfred Russel Wallace.

They met, here at Welney, and recreated Rowbottom's experiments with the floating barges. Objects swam around in the distance. It proved inconclusive. A second experiment was arranged – with three rafts spaced two miles apart, fixed with a target on each, so they could be sighted from the first to last. Through a theodolite, the middle marker was seen to be thirty-two inches higher than the others, due to the curve of the Earth, and as a result the planet's diameter was judged by Wallace to be 7,920 miles, which, by the way, is an astonishingly good calculation to be made by a theodolite and a piece of paper, seeing as modern computerised and laser guided methods measure the Earth's diameter to be only two and a half miles shorter than that.

Hampden wouldn't back down, however, and the argument went unresolved, both parties drawing different conclusions from what they saw through the crosshairs. Hampden refused to pay up, citing foul play on the grounds that the experiment had been different to the original one. The two Victorian gentlemen soon realised their beef was not with science, but with each other. They quickly escalated to a battle that almost came to fisticuffs and, eventually, a court case in 1876, which was so viciously toxic that the judges were careful not to rule on whether the Earth was flat or not, afraid they might be proved wrong. Instead they limited their judgement to the matter of whether or not the bet was valid. The argument between Hampden and Wallace rolled on, regardless, lasting sixteen years, causing several prosecutions for libel, and Hampden ending up in prison for calling Wallace 'a cheat, a swindler, an imposter and a thief.'

Heath and I looked down this same impressive stretch of water, and experienced some of Rowbottom's original sense of wonder. We stood on Welney Bridge, with the channel straight as a pin for six miles in both directions. Looking towards the north east, the dyke eventually vanished into a notch where a thin wedge of sky sank into the channel. When I borrowed Heath's pocket binoculars I saw, in that tiny horizon, a baffling mix of mirage and vapour and shadows. The air was muggy and humid, and the conditions perfect for the warping of optics, but nonetheless you fancied that at that distance, if only you could hold the binoculars steady enough, you might see China. Boats on the Yangtze, junks off Kowloon, pearl fishers off Japan. Perhaps, if the lenses were good enough, you might even glimpse the back of your own head, standing on Welney Bridge.

The Flat Earth Society was finally disbanded in the 1980s, due to an overwhelming body of evidence gleaned from several decades of space travel, global positioning satellites, astronomical science, views from plane windows and – it must be mentioned – common sense. But because all silly ideas have at least a second wag of the tail, the Flat Earth Society resurrected itself in 2005, now has its own website, and has been conducting a campaign to place a plaque on the bridge at Welney where, presumably, all its remaining members live.

'What do you think?' I asked Heath.

'The world's round,' he replied. 'But not here. Welney defies the curve. Here, the world is flat.'

Around us the landscape was relentlessly level. It was convincing.

'I also think,' Heath continued, 'we could have a go at the experiment ourselves. I like to imagine Samuel Rowbottom was a kind of avatar for you, and he stands for what you want to do on this journey of yours. He put himself in a landscape and wanted to challenge what he saw. He was looking for the not quite visible.'

So was this why Heath had brought me all the way to Welney?

'We have no rowing boat,' I said.

'Obviously. But you can ride your bike along the top of the bank. And I'll let you know if you vanish out there.'

'So I cycle along the flood bank and you watch from here?'

'I can call you on your mobile, when you disappear.'

Heath had the kind of look in his eye that shouldn't be challenged. He was clearly very keen that we might – once and for all – take the opportunity to solve the question of whether the Earth was round or flat. I thought I'd go along with the plan, and, as we needed to head north anyway, to return to our route, I set off down the riverbank. But as I cycled, I began to wonder what I was actually doing, and whether Heath's phone call to let me know *when I'd vanished* was somehow more emblematic of this landscape in general, and my increasing sense of feeling lost within it.

After half a mile or so, I came across a man in a hi-vis jacket working on a sluice gate. He'd exposed a concrete plinth and was measuring up a bolt that was going to be inserted. He was by himself, and it looked to be a pointless task. What difference would this bolt make in such a landscape, I thought? In what order were jobs organised? – at this rate his work might last a thousand years. I got off the bike and went over to him, and we talked for a while. He seemed absorbed in his task, and also in some meditative reverie for his place on the riverbank, in the sunshine, with the water quietly pooled alongside him. There was birdsong, a cuckoo calling from across the meadow, and a sound of insects humming over the channel. He finished measuring the bolt fixing, straightened his back and looked down the river, saying: 'Yep. It's a different world here.'

My mobile rang. When I answered it, Heath asked me what I was up to.

'I'm talking to a man fixing a bolt in concrete.'

'I can see that.'

'So you can still see me?'

'Will you be setting off on your bike soon?'

I looked back at Welney Bridge, and could clearly see Heath, still at the railings, watching me through the binoculars.

I set off again, riding on the riverbank path, and after about a mile I stopped to look back along the waterway. I could still see the bridge, so thought it was pointless to phone Heath. But as I rode further I began to think about Rowbottom's experiment, and how the man in the rowing boat must have felt, pulling the oars, wondering whether he was about to prove the Earth was flat, or not. A rowing boat seemed the appropriate means to prove this, because the rower would be looking back to where he came from at all times, and I thought of the Søren Kierkegaard quote that life is lived forwards, but can only be understood backwards.

I wondered whether I was vanishing from view out here. Were the baffling mixes of vapours and shadows rising round me, erasing me from the landscape? I had cycled for several miles; had I gone? I stopped the bike and stood on the path, looking back towards Welney, where I could see the tiny outlines of buildings and rooftops along the main street, but at the spot where I assumed Heath was, nothing was clear.

I called his mobile. 'Can you see me?' I asked.

'Try waving.'

I stood on the bank, waiving my jacket back and forth above my head.

'I don't know,' he said, after a while. 'I'm really not sure.'

I carried on waving, just in case.

Denver, in Utopia

I had cycled along the bank of the Old Bedford River into a strange land with strange names: Ten Mile Bank, Euximoor Drove, Apes Hall, Crabb's Abbey and Neep's Bridge. Here, they once built an experimental Hovertrain, because the land was so flat, and while I waited for Heath to catch up with me, I sat on one of the abandoned concrete plinths that had been used for the prototype track.

From my vantage point I looked across the fenland. Very little broke the view, but to the east I could see the massive silos, chimneys and processing units of the Wissington Sugar Beet factory, the largest of its kind in the world, which I've subsequently learnt can process three million tonnes of beet each year, all grown within a twenty-eight mile radius of the factory.

I watched Heath approach, his bike wobbling unsteadily on the path, and Half-Shandy getting shaken around in the basket. Heath seemed to be cycling almost too slowly to stay upright, and was making a straight path look very uneven.

'It's like the end of the world,' Heath said, when he finally arrived.

I wondered if he meant the fens in general or the industrial glory of the beet factory, with its apocalyptic swirls of smoke and steam, and its relentless manufacture of pure white sugar granules.

'Are you referring to sugar here, Heath?'

'Sugar?'

'A diet of too much sugar being the end of the world?'

'Well, I see your point, but no, I wasn't.'

We stared at the factory with its immense bulk – its chimney stack, its loading bays, its apron of cement surrounding it – looking as though the building itself had gorged on sugar.

'So that's one of the factories that's filling the nation's bellies with empty calories, rotting our teeth, and sending us to our sweet early graves of obesity and diabetes,' Heath said.

Hypocrite, I thought. Heath has a real weakness for sweet pastries. Especially Portuguese *natas* and *pastel de feijão*.

'But I meant the landscape in general,' he continued. 'The roads are dead straight, the fields are plumb level – every inch of it is ploughed and planted – even the rivers have been re-dug and re-laid. It's total. It's like man's finally got his wish and redrawn the world without its kinks and bumps. It's all very well being on a bike, because we're only passing through, but it must affect you to actually live here.'

He picked his bike up from the grass. 'With that in mind, shall we press on?'

We cycled off, and while I kept my eye on the footpath I was well aware of the emptiness of the fens pressing around me. Without doubt he was right.

Living round here must be a formidable challenge. The fenland winter must be an endurance, with boots permanently caked in mud, a perishing wind blasting the fields, and a steel-grey sky oppressing the land. Perhaps this is why so many people never travelled more than a cycle ride away from the place they were born in, with the result that this part of the fens is well known for it's own particular narrow-mindedness. Born in the fens, you stay in the fens; no one will arrive to replace you.

It's a good place to go mad, or to lock your mad away, and explains why asylums and sanatoriums have been built in this area throughout history. But like any truly empty space, it's also a place for revelation and insight. Many communities came to this area to nurture their own particular way of living. The Walloon and Huguenot protestants set up the Thorney and Sandtoft Colonies in the 1630s: there was the Newmarket Diggers Colony in 1650: The United Advancement Societies in Wisbech in the 1830s: the first Owenite community in Wretton in 1837: Chartists at Red Hall in 1848: Second World War pacifists set up by Max Plowman at Holton-Cum-Beckering in 1941: and self-funding smallholding communities at Cottenham, Lambourne, Fulney, Harrowby and Fen Drayton, running up to the last few years of the 20th century.

They all came here, attracted to an empty sky and an empty land, and no one to watch them thrive or fail. But the group I found most interesting during my research was the one at Manea Fen, where a Utopia was formed in 1838. The founding members wore Lincoln green and issued their own paper, *The Working Bee*, and Samuel Birley Rowbottom – he of the flat Earth argument – became one of its members. They built workshops, a windmill and a brickyard in order to form a small town of community cottages, all heated from a single source. The Manea Utopia even had its own floating church, St Withburga's – affectionately known as the *Fenland Ark* – that would come up the river every Sunday with enough seats for a congregation of thirty-four, blasting hymns out across the fen from its very own imported American organ, and raising a flag up a special pole so the boat's arrival would be seen over the tops of the riverbank.

Freedom and institutionalisation hand in hand, I think there's something sinister about a church that moves, picking up its congregation on the edges of fenland fields, realigning moral compasses with a dose of hymnal and sermon, then abandoning them to another week of huge sky and relentless wind.

As we cycled on, we began to appreciate just how many rivers and drainage channels were being brought together around us. From the south, the Ten Mile River brought the headwaters of the Great Ouse and its tributaries – the River Wissey, the Little Ouse and the River Lark – as well as the Old West River. From the south west came the manmade watercourses of the New Bedford River, the River Delph, and the Old Bedford River, straight and wide as a couple of runways. The Sixteen Foot Drain and the Middle Level Main Drain lurked half a mile away, across the fen from us, while sweeping round from the east came the engineering marvel of the thirty-five mile long Cut Off Channel, which shunts millions of tonnes of water backwards and forwards across the year, travelling under two rivers in vast U-bends along the way, to keep Ely dry in winter and the reservoirs of Essex wet in summer. All these flows and dykes and artificially swollen rivers had the single same destination as Heath and myself: the Denver Complex.

The Denver Complex might sound like a psychological disorder, but here it is a series of huge sluices that straddle the flow, making a barrier between all these freshwater rivers and the saline water of the Great Ouse. But despite the awareness of powerful liquid forces all around, giving the area a volcanic presence where everything might erupt at any moment, the Denver Sluice was a deceptively peaceful site. On one side was the weight of the combined fenland rivers, swollen beyond belief, and on the other, the deep gash of the tidal reach of the Great Ouse, with steep mud slicks down its banks and a pungent smell of seaweed, sixteen miles from the open sea. The sluice held the frontier, but it seemed to balance these forces calmly, and without effort. Heath and I leant our bikes against a fence, and he pointed out with relish a warning sign picturing just about every eventuality that might occur:

'Seems like a dangerous place,' he said. 'You do realise we're back on route.'

I wondered what he meant. 'We've just spent twenty miles on a tangent, Heath.'

'No. I was talking names. We left New York bound for California, and here we are in Denver. As in, Colorado.'

I admired Heath's knack for finding the positive in most situations. 'I see. And not a cowboy in sight.'

Around us we could hear a faint hum of electricity, and there was a sense that at any second a switch might be flicked and this giant apparatus of gates and sluices might fly apart, unleashing an end-of-the-world flood.

A house swept away by flood water near Denver Sluice in 1947.

There was nothing ornamental about the sluice. Its shape was designed to be functional, with five guillotine gates facing upriver, and two more guillotine gates and three mitred lock gates facing downriver. It seemed a complicated way of stopping a river's flow, partly achieved by raising and lowering vast steel plates, and partly achieved by those gates being pushed or pulled by the river itself. As we walked across, the giant wooden lock gates creaked like old ships' hulls beneath us, as the chains holding them rose and fell. A row of electric motors sat idly across the sluice, each one exposing innards of dark cogs and gears smothered in thick axle grease. The steel girders were covered in a grey-green patina that rubbed off like pigment on my fingers, and pigment is what it was: the colour of the river itself. Reaching the other side I noticed one of the stone abutments had a ground-to-parapet crack, as though the river's weight had playfully knocked the whole structure off its footings – a reminder of who's boss out here.

One of the 'Big Eye' gates was entirely seized up with the river's silt, and its steel guillotine had been replaced by an enormous concrete block. It reminded me of the way children try to dam streams on a beach – chucking a rock in one part of the flow, then trying to staunch the leaks by scooping sand around it, while the whole structure turns into a kind of porridge as the stream threads through.

I once stood on the Hoover Dam, where the two-hundred-mile length of Lake Mead presses on one side, while on the other there's nothing but empty air and a plunging canyon, with the Colorado River swirling at the bottom. There was a hum of electricity there too, but the dam's wall had a beautiful elegance, curved and sculpted to copy the physics of pressure it was built to overcome. Concrete built on a huge scale – but nonetheless following simple mathematical curves – can be incredibly beautiful, like the dome of the Pantheon in Rome, decreasing in thickness to allow a sky hole at the top, or a cooling tower that sweeps up from the ground like a breaking wave. Denver Sluice, in comparison, looked like a scrapyard of concrete and steel wedged into a river, and half giving up on the task of taming it.

Still, Heath looked pleased with it, and probably because it was – ultimately – a very honest structure: it blocked a river, and didn't need to be pretty. He likes that kind of functional design. The ramps of multi-storey car parks, for example, are something he admires. The one at the Grafton Centre in Cambridge winds down in one continual corkscrew from the top of the building to ground level, and descending it can lull you into an almost hypnotic dream state. Driving with him there is the only time I've ever heard Heath tell me he wished he owned a car.

As Heath wandered off down the riverbank, with Half-Shandy on a lead, a man came out of the control hut, wearing the high-tech neoprene jacket of the Environment Agency. After a brief chat, he told me the river was running nicely today. It seems like a confusing series of water channels round here, I said. He had bright blue eyes, and for a moment looked a little troubled. Oh yeah, he replied, it's not a physical job I've got, but I go home each night with a headache that I've got all the levels right. It's a puzzle. There's a three-metre drop in the tide some days. Perhaps he thought he'd offended the river, because he repeated how well it was behaving today. Then he pointed over the fields in the vague direction of Cambridgeshire: 'But I've got a right problem with the Cut Off Channel. When we've got plenty of water here we like to hold onto it. Open those gates and it just gets lost to the sea. But the problem is – today – they're down in Essex drawing water out the channel – they're pulling on it and I'm doing my best keeping it back.'

He said all this with great enthusiasm and a flicker of glee that he might be spoiling another man's day. I hadn't met someone who controlled rivers before, and it seemed like he carried his godly skills lightly. But I couldn't help imagining there was someone equally enthusiastic, equally bright blue-eyed, but also equally puzzled down in Essex, caught in a thirty-five mile tug-of-war, doing his damndest to draw the water while this man was at the Denver sluice raising and lowering lock gates trying to outfox him.

I went back onto the sluice, looking for Heath on the bank. As I leant against the steel girders I could hear the water making a strange gurgling sound below me, as though there was an old man down there sucking boiled sweets. I craned over the edge and saw, in the dark river, a series of large whirlpools. Each one was a tapering hole in the water, stretching down into the river like an animal's tail, but each hole big enough that an arm could reach down into it, right to the shoulder, and still not get wet. It was a sight that was mesmerising, and frightening, and I stared into these river holes thinking what would happen if they twisted together one day, uniting into one large braided rope of whirlpool, and whether this whirlpool would have such combined power that the whole sluice would be swallowed up, and after it the fens themselves, pulling into this vortex like a rough old carpet, vanishing into another plane of space and time that had so far remained beyond view.

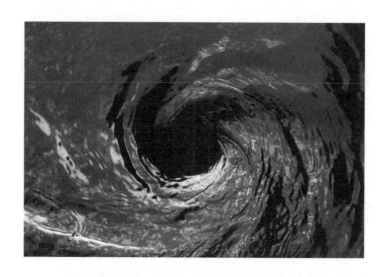

Lost in Space

North of Denver we came to the area where, over the space of a couple of miles, the road wound through the villages of Wiggenhall St Germans, Wiggenhall St Mary the Virgin, Wiggenhall St Peter and Wiggenhall St Mary Magdalen. I've always known the area as The Saints, and this was the area where I set some of my first novel, *Salt*. Little had changed since I last came here, nearly fifteen years ago. The villages are tiny, just a few houses either side of one of the several bridges that cross and re-cross the Great Ouse. And as Heath and I cycled along the small lane I remembered coming here when I was doing my initial research for the book: how I'd parked my car on the bridge at Wiggenhall St Germans and looked either way up the length of the great river passing beneath, wondering whether I had the time, the ability and the perspicacity to undertake and complete a novel partially set here. The tarmac on the bridge had felt gravelly, and I remember walking up to the rail hearing the sounds of my footsteps – the landscape was so quiet that day. Would I be able to sum this up? Would I be able to bring characters and story to this area? Would I fail?

Cycling through there again, with Heath in front of me and Half-Shandy looking back from his precarious basket, I felt oddly jubilant, that my writing had made a kind of full circle to return to this place – returning to the same area, but now with a new project that was partially revealing itself and partially concealing itself around me. The world seemed changed since I first came here – it seemed faster, more complicated, and more uncertain, and I felt aware of all the passing years in myself, too. But the spirit of writing felt fresh and inspired, and the jubilation came partly from experiencing that moment all books feel, where ideas begin to unfold around you. Look in every direction, and the narrative is there, waiting.

As the light began to fade we checked in at the Premier Inn near Kings Lynn, which was built next to a roundabout on the A17. They had a no pet policy, so Heath circumvented that by carrying Half-Shandy into his room zipped up in a holdall, which is why a whippet is such a conveniently sized dog to own. To me, the holdall looked suspiciously dog shaped, with Half-Shandy's long snout clearly prominent and trying to sniff the air at the corner of the zip, but no one at the reception seemed to notice.

In my room I lay on the bed and looked up at the ceiling for a while. We were back on the A17, at least, but the Premier Inn was a strange place to call a home for the night, built next to a Shell petrol station, a McDonald's drive-through and a roundabout. My room looked homely enough, but anonymous too, and I was caught feeling somewhere in-between, as though I was stuck within an orbit of places I didn't really understand. On one side of the hotel was a view across a field of head-high brambles to the large rectangular shape of the East Coast Storage warehouse, and on the other – the view from my window – was of the roundabout where the A17 met the A47. A spill of light came from the Shell station next door, across an apron of tarmac, and the roundabout was lit with a circle of bright sodium streetlamps. Everywhere beyond was as dark as the sea.

Don't think too much, I advised myself, which is generally good advice in places like this.

After Heath had settled Half-Shandy in his room, we met in the foyer and walked across the car park to the Brewers Fayre, next door. The night smelt of vegetables and car exhausts, and at the entrance of the restaurant there was an added smell of fried cooking and carpets.

Heath read the menu by the door, and immediately looked defeated. I saw names listed as *Combo Feast*, *Loaded Nachos*, *Smothered Chicken* and *Oreo Cookie Pie*. The chicken was described as 'smothered in BBQ sauce, topped with bacon and melted cheddar cheese. Served up with a pineapple ring, chips, corn on the cob and coleslaw.' I imagined layers and layers of food, and a process of digging through its formidable strata with a trowel, each layer promising some kind of culinary treat, but all of them fundamentally burying the dish itself in a kind of calorific insulation. There seemed to be a lot of food and nothing to eat at the same time. Further down the list I spotted a dish called *Hand Battered Giant Atlantic Cod*, as if some mortal struggle had been involved in bringing that huge fish to the plate, and it might be served across the whole table top.

'What are we going to do?' I asked Heath.

'To think that we're in the most fertile agricultural land in England,' he replied. 'All those asparagus and kale fields out there, and in here all we can get are nachos.'

'I once saw squirrel on a menu in Lincolnshire,' I said.

'That – is something I'd consider right now.'

Wondering what might happen, we stepped into the restaurant, and stood next to a slowly revolving shelving unit displaying the desserts. An empty plate was labelled *Dirty Mud Pie*, and came into view every ten seconds. A man came out of the toilet, using two walking sticks, and behind him I could see a windowless room with the sound of Phil Collins' *One More Night* being piped through on speakers. On the other side of the corridor space was a slot machine, based on Noel Edmunds' game show *Deal or No Deal*. A button with *Take Streak* written on it was surrounded by six neurotically flashing portraits of Noel Edmunds himself, winking at me like a neon demon.

'Shall we see what's on sale at the petrol station?' I suggested.

A few minutes later we were in the groceries aisles of the Shell station, standing in front of a shelf of crisps and snack bars, when Heath suddenly said:

'I feel...' and he seemed to struggle for the right way to start '...struck by an overwhelming truth. It's certain – *certain*, that humans will die out. I think I always knew this, but it's only just occurred to me how close we are. There are too many people for the world to feed – it's out of control. Did you know there are an extra two hundred thousand people on the planet *each day*? At this rate we probably only have – what – a hundred and fifty to two hundred years left. That's eight generations.'

He gave out a little sigh, and wandered off towards a Wild Bean coffee machine. When we queued up to pay at the till, he turned to me and whispered: 'We've run out of history. It's the end game of the Anthropocene. We may as well fill the oceans with plastic, and burn all the fossil fuels. There's no legacy to worry about.'

I nodded, and decided not to say anything. Heath had made himself upset.

'The problem is,' he whispered, 'compared with other animals – we're actually a very average mammal. An average mammal with a huge ego.'

'Which pump are you?' the cashier asked.

'We're – on foot,' I replied.

The cashier looked confused, and stared through the window across the forecourt.

We ate egg and cress sandwiches in Heath's room, while Half-Shandy sat on the carpet between us, gnawing a cheese pasty.

'We survived,' I said.

'Yes. A long day. Odd at times. Was that Phil Collins being played in the toilets at the restaurant?'

I nodded. 'I once taught on a writing course in Shropshire,' I added, 'and the one afternoon I hiked through the forest to the next village and there, in a windowless public toilet, *Phantom of the Opera* was being played on loud speakers. It was very strange. I remember the toilet was decked out in steel sheeting, like some kind of military installation. When I stepped out I stood in the sunshine and looked back at it, wondering whether it had really happened.'

Late at night, feeling unsettled, I walked down to the bank of the Great Ouse, which was only a hundred yards from the Premier Inn. I felt like I'd reached the edge of the fens, and that behind me were miles and miles of sticky mud that had the ability to suck anything down into them, and leave no trace. I thought of my mother, trying to reveal the secrets of fenland soil at her laboratory desk, then thought of my grandfather pushing bulbs into the mud with his wellington boots, the American bombs sinking into the marsh at Gedney, and King John's dazzling crown jewels vanishing into quicksand. The area swallows up its secrets: bombs and crown jewels and even family histories can vanish and never be found again. The vortexes beneath the Denver Sluice were spinning, still spinning, like open mouths swallowing it all.

In front of me, the river flowed thickly and without definition, deep in its channel of slimy black estuary mud. It smelt sharp and sour and full of salt, and I thought what a powerful presence a river is at night, passing by with such impenetrable volume, but something that couldn't quite be seen. Wasn't this what I was looking for, I reminded myself? Crossing East Anglia searching for the not quite visible. Did this moment sum it up – to sit on a dark riverbank and feel the presence of something immeasurable passing in front of me?

The plan was to continue in a relatively straight line across East Anglia, following the A47 to California but, standing by the bank of the Great Ouse, my eel-sense of migration was telling me to change my direction. The eel follows the river to the sea, retracing a route until it arrives at its birthplace. And like the eel, my own journey across East Anglia was one of personal return. The route to California was a straight one, but a detour to North Norfolk – where I grew up – was the route that was calling me.

When I got back to my room I watched TV for a while. There was a programme about a nightclub in Ibiza, but it felt like a transmission being beamed into this room from a distant planet. I recognised the colours and patterns on the screen, but they didn't seem to apply to where I was, currently, lost in space. I switched it off and thought again about the Giant Atlantic Cod, lurking in the freezers of the Brewers Fayre next door, like some mythical beast in a morgue, lured from its hiding place in the North Atlantic to a chest freezer in a red brick building on a semi-industrial unit on the outskirts of Kings Lynn. How did it end up here? How did I, also, end up at this place tonight?

I slept badly, next to a roundabout that seemed to be spinning its cars and trucks around like a washing machine. It felt like I was trying to sleep by the side of a vortex, a slowly turning, never fading whirlpool that might yet drag me down.

Bangers

'I think it might do us good,' Heath announced, over his continental breakfast, 'to see a glimpse of how things will be at the end of time.'

'Where?'

'Near here.'

'This morning?'

'It begins at eleven.'

Heath felt in no rush to explain, or was trying to make me guess. He was enjoying his croissant, and I don't think I'd seen him this happy for a couple of days. Perhaps sleeping next to a roundabout had suited him.

'Sleep well?' I asked.

'Like a log.'

'Half-Shandy?'

'Not a murmur.'

He handed me a flyer he'd picked up from the reception. 'Stock car racing,' he said. 'Wilfully smashing cars – like we're hurrying up the end of civilisation. What's not to like?'

I was surprised by this, because Heath doesn't like cars, doesn't own a car, and doesn't like the fact that I *do* own a car. He was in an unpredictable mood.

'You seem very cheery this morning?' I said.

'Pleasure comes from pastries.'

We arrived at the Adrian Flux arena, south of Kings Lynn, in good time. As we cycled in through the gates we could hear a full-throttled roar of cars coming from behind the stands, and the air had a gritty feeling of soil and smoke, laced with smells of chip vans and petrol. We possibly went in the wrong entrance, because we suddenly found ourselves in a muddy car park surrounded by dozens of crews prepping their vehicles, revving engines, changing tyres, and whacking lump hammers into wheel arches. There was a lot of frantic noise with engines pushed to screaming point, and mechanics emerging from clouds of fumes wiping hands on their overalls. It looked as though a scrapyard was simultaneously being pulled apart and reassembled. In the middle of all this, the cars themselves sat like vicious animals – growling and snapping, like they were being prodded to make them snarl, and I naturally felt a bit scared and out of place, suspecting a stock car might suddenly lurch forward off its wheel jacks and bite me like a wild dog.

The cars were brightly painted, stripped of their windows and dented all over. Most had the nicknames of their drivers painted on their sides, like 'Fat Boy,' 'Baino,' 'Trailer Trash,' 'Pistol Pete,' 'Shaggy,' 'Jooble,' and 'Spud.'

Yet in all this noise I soon began to see small moments of calm. By the side of one of the cars I saw a long-haired child in a boiler suit writing *Donny*, as carefully as a sign painter, onto a door panel.

Nearby – amid the angle grinding of the bodywork and the hammering of the wheel arches – I saw a car mysteriously levitating over the oil puddles. When I looked closer, I noticed the car was owned by an all female crew called *The Girlies*, and, at the back, one of the drivers – squatting like a weightlifter – seemed to be raising the car with superhuman strength as she changed a wheel. The car rocked perilously in the air above her, defying gravity, until she pulled off the wheel and I spotted that the car was pivoted on a hidden jack.

Passing these sights we made our way to the grandstands – which were really just a few rows of cement steps behind crash barriers and a sturdy wire fence. In front of us was a circular dirt track that looked as though it had been ground down by a tornado. A PA system echoed around the stands, calling out numbers and drivers and generally whipping up excitement, although there were probably only a couple of hundred people scattered about, and most of them in brightly coloured mechanic's overalls.

In a programme, I saw a list of *intriguing* races through the year, from *Reliant Robins Battle of Britain*, to *Banger Battle of the Sexes*, *Unlimited Banger War of the Worlds*, *Dirt Quake* and *2 litre (Non Mondeo) King of the Fens*.

On 29th October there was going to be:

HALLOWEEN CARNIVAL NIGHT

Unlimited Banger Spooktacular!

A line of cars drove onto the track and, after a slow processional lap where they revved their engines, they suddenly roared into speed, charging round the circuit in a cloud of acrid smoke, their tyres spitting up dirt at each other and occasionally barging each other off at the corners, making the spectators cheer each time. The noise was deafening, and although Heath and I tried to follow the race, we both felt disorientated and dizzy with the circular flow of angry metal in front of us, where there didn't seem to be a clear winner or loser or any particular lap count. Parts of the race began to vanish in the clouds of exhaust and dust, the aggression out there seemed uncontainable as if it might whirl out of control in the spin, and then among the cars I briefly glimpsed the name *Donny*, where it had been painted below the driver's window.

Quite suddenly the race came to an end and the tannoy system barked out a result, before going on to draw attention to various outrageous manoeuvres that perhaps we should have spotted. The noise of the engines dropped and the cars limped out at a crawl, several of them steering drunkenly where collisions had bent the metalwork onto their wheels.

Heath was excited: 'Wasn't that fantastic!' he said. 'Don't you like the way they smashed everything up? All those cars that were once gleaming in the showroom. Think of all that work, all that design and manufacture, and all the people who saved up to buy those cars after seeing the pictures in a catalogue, then washed and waxed them every Sunday – just to end up with them being crashed to pieces in a pointless circuiting of a pointless track in a pointless sport. It's brilliant.'

'What's brilliant?'

'The German's have a wonderful expression for it. It goes like this: *Alles hat ein Ende, nur die Wurst hat zwei.* Everything has an end. Only the sausage has two.'

I didn't really know what to think.

I saw this woman's hand holding the wire fence, a gold coin ring on each of her fingers, except the little finger, which wore a ring with the word BITCH on it.

The final race was a surprise: from a previously hidden entrance twelve hearses drove onto the track in a procession which, maybe intentionally, resembled a grim cortege, with engines growling and revving ominously. One of the hearses had a rough plywood coffin bolted to its roof with the name of the driver written along its side. They drove a lap of honour, slowly, blaring their horns, each car with its windows knocked out and the side panels dished in, painted with numbers and outlines of skulls and tombstones and cartoon bats, and words written in the dripping blood font of Hammer House films. All very much tongue-in-cheek, and the crowd greeted the grisly parade with extra humour, pointing out the jokes written on the bodywork, or the drivers, some of whom seemed to be in fancy dress.

The drivers' names – GONZO, SCULLY, ELLIOTT or TED – were painted on the hearses, where once flower arrangements had spelt out the names of the dead. I thought it must be a strange and unsettling experience to write your own name on a hearse.

It was a world away from the job these vehicles had once done: each one carrying the austere, dark shine of wood among the bright blooms of flowers, in spaces where, now, there was a hollowed-out emptiness. These hearses – once beautifully maintained Daimlers and Humbers – now had their headlights removed, and had been given the empty socketed look of skulls themselves. Just how many bodies had this combined cortege carried? Just how many of the dead had passed through these vehicles, while the wheels had turned softly on churchyard gravel and the undertakers had stared forward with impassive profiles. Some of the drivers were dressed in funeral suits, but as the hearses increased their speed, beginning to circle the track with a souped-up roar, it was easier to imagine the cadavers themselves were now at the wheel.

The dust rose, the hearses began to jostle and knock each other at the corners, and in fractured glimpses into the hollowed out cabs, behind the visors of crash helmets and ski goggles, I was reminded of the Mexican *Dia de los Muertos* on November 1st each year, where entire villages dress as the dead and dance in the cemeteries through the night in a ragged drunken carnival, until the point near dawn where the living and the dead can hardly be separated.

Once, on a trip to Sicily, I drove to the mountain top village of Savoca, famous for its tradition of mummifying the most important members of its community. The grizzly horde was kept below the Capuchin monastery, in a narrow crypt at the bottom of a long flight of steps. I left my three-year-old son at street level in a café with my mother, before descending into the crypt. The mummified corpses were arranged around the walls, standing or leaning in recesses in the plaster. There were many of them, and it was difficult not to feel that these men (for I don't recollect any women making it in to the display) faced you with fixed expressions of resentment. No doubt they'd agreed to being mummified before they'd died, which must have involved visits from the mortician, choices about which clothes they'd be dressed in, monies paid to buy the best alcove on the wall, and general agreements about the poses they wanted to express for the rest of time. The mummies had 18th- and 19th-century clothing on, jackets and breeches and occasionally tricorn hats, now very much faded and moth-eaten, as though they'd been dressed in rags rather than their most expensive finery. Bones poked through, emerging at the wrists. A hand had fallen off here and there, to be left on the floor of the display cabinets. Other body parts had found their way into an ossuary of miscellaneous knuckles and vertebrae in the corner. Trousers hung like flags around the stick-like bones. The corpses had the air of a tragic community, all of whom had made the same mistake, the only consolation for some being that others had decayed at a more calamitous rate, sinking down through the remains of their clothes to form little cairns of disconnected bones on top of silver buckled shoes. Time itself had given them a pantomime look, a dusty theatricality that seemed absurdly pompous. How had they thought they could cheat death by presenting themselves this way? And as I'd looked I'd been struck by an overriding certainty – that in all of their faces, where the greyed leather of old skin had withered, or fallen away entirely, revealing parts of jaw and teeth and eye sockets, each had had a look of complete and overwhelming agony.

A Fenland Walrus

After the stock car racing, Heath and I walked through the nearby Saddlebow industrial estate. It was an untidy area, made up of individual units including a haulage truck repairer, a paper factory and an agrifluids supplier. The road was muddy and the gutters were choked with plastic rubbish and engine oil. I think we must have been reeling from all the noise of the racetrack, because we walked in silence and let Half-Shandy trot along the road in front of us, his tail tucked up nervously under his belly.

The road ended in a patch of waste ground where abandoned streetlamps stood among a thicket of briars. A couple of hundred yards away we saw the rectangular outline of the King's Lynn gas power station, with enormous pipes sticking out from its sides, as if a child had built a robot, using a cardboard box and toilet rolls wrapped in tin foil. Next to it was the equally angular concrete shape of the Relief Channel Sluice. Ordinarily, Heath would have been keen to take a closer look at these structures, eulogising about functional architecture and its connection to the land that surrounds it, but his mood had become contemplative again, and he seemed unduly subdued.

We climbed the flood bank and sat on the grass, looking across the large muddy width of the Great Ouse. Here, near its outlet into the Wash, hugely swollen with spring-coils of tidal water, the river looked mistrustful. All that drainage of the land, feeding this leviathan river, and just a few miles away the sea rolling up against it, waiting for a chance to flood inland.

'Are you alright?' I asked.

Heath stared across the river at the slicks of mud and seaweed on the other side. 'I think I might let you do the next stage of the journey by yourself.'

'Really? Why's that?'

'I should get back to Cambridge. You know – various loose ends.'

'Can't Cambridge wait?'

'Oh, I'm sure it can – it doesn't do much other than wait. But me, I'm beginning to feel that if I don't sit at my desk for a while, and if I don't cross Midsummer Common and see how the walnuts are doing on the tree there, then I lose my bearings. I've been a couple of days away – it's made me anxious.'

'Well, we all feel like that, Heath.' He didn't reply, and I knew his decision had probably already been made. 'I knew you were feeling odd,' I added.

'Why?'

'You've not even mentioned the sluice gate over there. Or the power station.'

'Yes, a dead giveaway,' he said, brightly. 'Well, while I'm here, it would be churlish not to have little peep at them, wouldn't it?'

He stood up, brushed the dirt from his trousers, and walked off down the footpath to get a closer look. I watched him approach a chain-link fence, where he stopped to read a notice. Always attracted to the periphery, to the overlooked, trying to make connections between the unconnected. He makes an odd journey across the planet, I thought.

Looking across the huge brown width of the Great Ouse, I contemplated the possibility of having to do the rest of the journey by myself. Heath's decision felt sudden, and I was worried that he'd regretted coming on this trip. I would miss him. Journeys are most intense alone, but most enjoyable shared. Although he'd been a little maddening at times, I was used to having him around. But I wouldn't try to persuade him out of it, I decided. And without him, I'd be free to go to North Norfolk, where my migratory compass was already re-directing me.

Among the muddy swirls of the river was the occasional piece of driftwood, floating swiftly, and I was abruptly reminded of some research I once did, where I came across an account of a walrus that had once swum up

the Great Ouse. I imagined how the walrus must have looked down there –
its head the size of a blacksmith's anvil, but with stiff whiskers and a couple
of ivory tusks, then pictured it trying to haul its body out on the mud slicks
that shelve steeply into the river, or perhaps gnawing through the planks of
a rotten jetty. Messing around in a fenland river, thousands of miles from its
North Atlantic colony, finding its way here in a similarly odd route to the one
the *Giant Atlantic Cod* took to the Brewers Fayre's chest freezer. A walrus,
in Lincolnshire. It seemed truly improbable, and despite several subsequent
trawls on Google I have never in fact found this account again. It's strange
how the Internet does this: conjuring a picture, and then concealing it. It has
a cloudlike aspect, allowing us to glimpse something extraordinary through
a gap in the vapour, but sometimes never finding it again.

So a walrus may or may not have swum up the Great Ouse at this point,
confusing itself, those who saw it from the riverbanks, and me glimpsing it
through the fog of the Internet, but as I looked at the impenetrably thick
flows and eddies and swirls of the river beneath me, I knew the true secrets
of any given landscape will always be hidden from view.

Heath and I went back to our Travelodge and, in the car park, beside a peculiar sign, I outlined my plan for the next stage of the journey. The night before, sitting by the Great Ouse, I'd decided to cycle up to the North Norfolk coast and, leaving the bike there, walk all the way to Cromer.

'The North Norfolk coast's not the direct route to California,' I explained, 'but without going along it I don't think I'll be able to *truly* arrive at California.'

'I understand,' Heath said. 'And therefore it is on the way to California – perhaps not geographically, but mentally.'

'Exactly.' The car park of the Travelodge, with its neatly arranged bays, sensible kerbing and patronising signposting seemed an appropriate place to voice this type of thinking.

'Have you heard of the Oyster Stone at Cockley Cley?' he asked.

'No.'

'Only, I might stop off and see if I can find it, on the way back to Cambridge.'

I thought I'd leave it at that – Heath was beginning to sound a little eccentric.

'But I did think I'd return for the last leg of the route, if I may? Shall we meet in Cromer?' he said.

'Yes – of course.' I was pleased he wanted to return, and finish the job we'd set out to do. 'How about under the pier in... let's say two days' time?

'Sunday at three?'

'Yep. Sunday at three.' I liked the way Heath made arrangements. Despite having a mobile, he prefers to plan things the old fashioned way. He's always said mobiles have made meeting up more complicated.

'Till the pier, then.' Heath began to wheel his bike towards the exit. He stopped, then brought the bike back towards me.

'Just had a thought,' he said. 'Want to take the dog with you?'

PART TWO

ALONG THE EDGE

The Whale

In January 2016, sperm whales began to wash up along the North Sea coasts. There were thirty in total, from a bachelor pod that should have been in the deep ocean areas of the Atlantic, or off the Norwegian coast, gorging on a diet of squid and octopus. But for some reason they veered into the North Sea where they soon found themselves in shallow waters, and quickly began to starve. They had no food and – as this large group worked their way down towards Germany and the Low Countries – fewer and fewer ways out. They became dehydrated. Two washed ashore on the German island of Helgoland, and ten more at Friedrichskoog, Busum, Wangerooge and at the mouth of the Weser. Six became stranded on the Dutch island of Texel, and one in France, at Hemmes de Marck. The dwindling pod of sperm whales was spotted off the North Norfolk coast where one – a lone male – became beached under the cliffs at Hunstanton. Another foundered on the beach at Skegness, and one more found its way to Wainfleet, where it was washed ashore near the bombing range at Gedney Drove End. Two more continued the journey, floundering among the sandbanks of the Wash until they became stranded at Gibraltar Point, on the Lincolnshire coast. A drone took an iconic bird's eye view photograph of them lying side by side on the sand, perfectly parallel, as if they were performing a synchronised manoeuvre at the moment of their death, like a supersized *danse macabre*.

Two weeks later a final surviving whale washed up, alive, at Hunstanton. What it had done out there for that fortnight in January, knowing that the last five of its pod had already died on the nearby sandbanks, was unknown. Their death throes must have echoed across the Wash and this last one must have listened to them. The whale finally beached itself only two miles from one of the other strandings, which may have been deliberate.

I watched this dying whale on TV. Local people doused it with buckets of water, and when the tide came in it partially floated, before rolling on its side, its blowhole blasting like a cannon, and its great tail thrashing behind it. Everyone knew it would die, and the whale knew it, too.

Altogether, several thousand people went to visit these dead whales, and their bodies – specifically the Lincolnshire strandings near Skegness – became covered with graffiti. A CND badge was sprayed on one of the flanks, and a rather bizarre 'Mans Fault' was painted onto a raised tail fluke. The evidence in fact points to man not being to blame for this bachelor pod beaching themselves, and the missing apostrophe in the slogan bothered me also: wrong to write on a whale in the first place, wrong to assume it was man's fault, and wrong to miss the apostrophe, too.

Oddly, of the whales washed up that year, only the one stranded at Wainfleet was left untouched, due to it being on a Royal Air Force bombing range. Not blowing it up because it was surrounded by unexploded ordinance was ironic. I suspect that once the media lenses were turned away, this whale may even have become one of the range's more unusual targets.

Just before they'd died, each of the six whales had unfurled a six-foot penis onto the soft sand. These whales die in a moment of ecstasy, it seems. I thought of all those many thousands of people who visited those whales, taking their children with them, murmuring sadly about what a tragic sight it was, and realised they'd all been flashed at – by creatures endowed with the largest cocks on the planet. The sperm whale's penis is not something you can ignore.

I phoned my brother and we talked about what had driven the whales to beach themselves. There was a theory gaining traction that a solar storm had interrupted their navigation, but he didn't think much of that. He also thought the whales were too canny to be trapped in the North Sea hunting elusive squid, too sensible to follow a deranged pod leader; and he didn't have much truck with the idea that they'd been misled by the sonar of one of our ridiculous, nonsensical, pointless sabre-rattling Trident nuclear submarines. And why – I asked – did they have the habit of dying with their penises hanging out? Yes, I wondered that, too, he replied. His theory was that, after all the rocky coasts of the North Atlantic, these rude boys had decided to masturbate in the soft sands off East Anglia – dragging their willies across the fine silt ridges of the Wash until – getting carried away – they failed to notice the tide had gone out.

'Remember the Brancaster whale,' he said.

'Ah – yes, that was a pretty rude sight, too.'

Twenty-five years before this conversation with my brother, he and I had visited our own sperm whale that had just washed ashore at Brancaster, on the North Norfolk coast. We visited it on a wintry day and when we arrived at the beach, all we could see was a single black shape sticking out from the edge of a sandbank, a quarter of a mile out to sea. The whale was unreachable, remote and mysterious, and seemed to be locked in battle with the waves like a ship being wrecked. A few days later it washed up dead on the beach. We returned and this time found it lying among the bands of shingle and sand. It looked deflated, flattened by its own weight, as black as burnt rubber.

We were the only people on the beach that day, and as we approached the whale, its sheer size became apparent. As long as a London bus, lying on its side but still taller than I was, it had seemed too large to be a single living thing. The whole area reeked of its decay and from its belly a large gash had been made through which a confusing goo of grey blubber and flesh had partially escaped. Its penis lolled away to the side, with the tip dug into the sand. My brother and I stared at that for quite some time feeling – well – rather impressed by it. The whale's skin – particularly across the head – was covered with deep scars that might have come from fights with giant squid. The tail was as wide as a rowing boat, elegantly shaped and sharp edged, made of a thickly smooth skin that was as hard as mahogany. And inside its mouth was a row of gleaming ivory teeth – each one fitting into its own perfect socket on the upper jaw. What we never found was the eye, although we climbed on top of the whale and walked up and down its length, with the dense body bowing ever so slightly beneath us. Mystery was the overriding sensation of that day. A whale that was baring all, but also indecipherable.

I tried to imagine aspects of that whale's life: how it must have felt to lift such a magnificent tail and be thrust down through the water. Or the distant beat of a great heart. The feeling of impregnable skin encircling you. What were the lines of magnetism and migration that you would understand, the navigation that you could follow, the topography of underwater ridges and gullies that formed your map? What was it like to feel the pressure of a thousand metres of water on your back, and charge open-mouthed into a thicket of giant tentacles, not knowing whether you'd survive?

An encounter with a whale has been the unlocking of creative thought across the centuries, and seeing that sperm whale was certainly a seminal moment for me, and perhaps the moment I decided to be a writer. Albrecht Dürer journeyed to a stranded whale in Zeeland, during December 1520, in order to draw it. From his 'Memoirs of Journeys to Venice and the Low Countries' he wrote:

> At Zierikzee in Zeeland a whale has been washed ashore by a great tide and storm; it is much more than a hundred fathoms long; no one in Zeeland has ever seen one even one-third as long, and the fish cannot get off the land. The people would be glad to see it gone, for they fear the great stink, for it is so big they say it could not be cut in pieces and the oil got out of it in half a year.

But before Dürer could see his whale, it washed out to sea again and, as a result, the world is missing that particular Dürer engraving from its art galleries.

The North Norfolk Council has the habit of disposing of beached sperm whales by studding them with explosives, like cloves in an orange, and blowing them up. I don't know why they do this. They blew up the Brancaster whale, and several months later my brother and I made our third and final visit. All that were left were parts of the skull and jawbones. We went at night, and I remember sitting within the walls of the skull where they wrapped around my back like the car of a fairground waltzer. I was there, in a natural windbreak, where just a few months earlier the largest brain that has ever existed on the planet had been. Inside the skull was an eerie place. In front of me – dimly lit – was one of the huge maxillae jawbones. That night my brother and I dragged a length of it from the beach, with the notion of having it stand in our back yard at his house in Norwich, like one half of the famous whalebone arch at Whitby, or those on the Isle of Lewis or the Falklands. Our bone was about five feet long, as flat as a church pew, and seemed to weigh a ton. We carried it in the boot of his car and, back in Norwich, tried to dry it out in front of an open fire in the living room, which proved to be a mistake. Leaning against the mantelpiece throughout the night, the bone began to boil and weep whale fat. The house took on the qualities of a rendering blockhouse on a 19th-century Hull whaler. In my memory the air had a greasy, honeyish glow – and it can't have been far off this – as we were eventually driven out of the house by the smoke and the stench. From the safety of the back yard we looked through the window at the sperm whale's steaming jawbone leaning against the fireplace, wondering what kind of smoky hell we'd created.

We'd turned this experience with the Brancaster whale into a nightmarish thing, as men so often do, ruining the things that we most value. The dead whale had affected us both, and we'd wanted to hold onto it, but had further vandalised it instead. We destroy the things we want to save; we all do. Eventually we carried that stickily oozing jawbone out into the yard and leant it against the wall, where it remained for a long time, and where people may have thought it was a length of chipboard from the back of a sofa. At some point during the last twenty years someone climbed over the wall and stole it, and its journey continued. The final end point for the last piece of that sperm whale is now another mystery.

The five-foot-long jawbone was not the only thing my brother and I plundered that day from Brancaster beach. We also found a colossal fish, brought in on the same tide. It was a giant sunfish, measuring perhaps four feet from top to bottom – one of the oddest fish in the sea, because it is all face and no tail, is flat and shiny as a coin and, if you turn it head on towards you, it virtually disappears. We'd never seen such an extraordinary fish on a Norfolk beach before, so we decided – as we did with the whale jawbone – to take it back in the boot of his car to Norwich. We called the fish Murco, after the local petrol station in Brancaster. Our idea was that we would get it stuffed, but even on the way back to Norwich we realised what a fool's undertaking this already was. The fish was too large, too thinly skinned, too ready to start smelling. That night we left it draped over the edges of the dining room table, and decided we'd take it first thing in the morning to the taxidermist on Elm Hill.

Aspects of this event are lost to me now, such as how we carried such a giant fish up the length of a busy street, and how those who saw us reacted. But I do remember our reflection in the Oxfam window, where the fish had briefly seemed to be swimming once more, several feet in the air. I also recall the taxidermist meeting us at his open door, with a mixture of puzzlement and barefaced suspicion. Who were these two brothers, bracing an enormous fish between them? What was the trick being played? Curiosity won out, and we were invited in, where we laid the monster on his worktable and talked about the possibility of having it stuffed. He touched the skin with the flat of a palette knife, and rubbed his chin, full of admiration for such a strange creature, but probably at a loss as to how to deal with it, or the two of us. The fish seemed to fill most of his shop, its tiny mouth set in a tight grimace. I remember starting to stroke the taxidermist's cat – the same one that that always sat in his shop window. That cat used to sit there all day, perfectly motionless between the other stuffed animals, and then it would shock the life out of you when it suddenly raised a paw to clean itself. Sometimes it would gaze at the taxidermist's workbench, where a conveyor belt of animals turned up to be skinned, dismembered, rearranged and sown up again. Surely it was only a matter of time before this cat, too, would join the queue? Each day it regarded the taxidermist impassively, with an expression that cats have totally nailed, giving nothing away.

We gave the glorious sunfish to the taxidermist to do with it as he pleased. But it was clearly an animal that couldn't be stuffed. For us it was the disappointing end to another marvellous object we'd found on a Norfolk beach. We never saw it stuffed in his display window. Nor, among his display animals, did I ever see his cat, despite looking out for it for several years.

As Half-Shandy and I walked across Brancaster beach, beginning our journey along the coast to Cromer, there was no remnant of the sperm whale I'd once seen there. Or the sunfish. But their absence was just as powerful: this beach now had a loaded dimension. The whale may have gone, but I still *felt* its presence. I sat on the sand, with Half-Shandy running along the high tide line. I thought about my journey so far, and how so much of it had been following a map of phantoms that were only loosely attached to landscape – such as childhood memories, or the glimpses in my grandfather's photos – all of them feeling similarly distant and unreliable. In the journey across the fens there seemed to be a common strand: a walrus that may or may not have been seen, King John's vanished treasure, a village where a murder took place, a house where a black dog was left – most of what I'd been looking for had been tantalisingly hidden.

I hoped to be on more certain ground now, because this was Norfolk, my home county, the land that formed me – but even here on Brancaster beach I was already expecting to find a similar set of false turns and dead ends.

Scolt Head

This part of the North Norfolk coast is a confusing maze of rising and submerging sandbanks, steep-sided channels and shallow mud flats. Water can rise round your feet in a matter of minutes as the tide brings a soft foam of brackish water that works its way through the capillaries of creeks that dissect the saltmarsh. With each hour that passes, the map has to be redrawn. A sandbank seen a second ago is suddenly rippling water, then gone, and when the next low tide comes it may have shifted a few feet this way or that. An inlet of calm flat water can drain to reveal a semi-industrial wasteland of mud slicks and gullies, pockmarked with shingle beds and pools. An empty twist of creek might suddenly become a line of old staithe posts, each one like a cruel, dark tooth stuck out of the mud, or a line of oyster nets where the shells crackle and fizz in the air. Mud can be hard and brittle as toffee, as soft as porridge or slick as double cream. It's a place where you quickly have to learn a new method of getting about, and you often learn this the hard way, when you're stuck up to your knees in black oily mud, or fallen flat on your front.

There are few true islands off Norfolk but, twice a day, Scolt Head is one of them. It is three miles long and half-a-mile in width, made up of grassy banks and a crest of sand dunes. Facing out to sea, its beach has fine white sand covered with razor shells and the occasional seal. It lies off Burnham Deepdale and Burnham Overy Staithe, separated from the coast by a channel which – at low tide – takes a couple of minutes to cross, over the exposed mud and sand. When Half-Shandy and I reached one of the crossing points on Norton Creek, it was fairly late in the day, and we had timed it poorly, because the water was already rising in front of us. I guessed we had twenty minutes or so to make the crossing, so I picked Half-Shandy up and carried him across, with my bags strapped to my back. The water was never more than knee deep, but even as I walked out onto the hard sand of Scolt Head on the other side I could feel a door was closing behind me as the sea began to flood the channel with force. I set Half-Shandy down and he scampered off towards the dunes, unaware that he and I were effectively shipwrecked for the next twelve hours.

Stranding yourself is wonderful. The sea has come in and cut this part of Norfolk away. Swimming back is certainly not something you should try in the first two hours after the change of a high or low tide, when the water flows faster than a person can swim and can double with power in a matter of minutes. The flat sea masks a seabed riddled with gullies and creeks, and through these hidden channels the water races with hidden speed – rip tides almost impossible to spot on the surface, that can twist round your ankles like ropes and pull you down.

I pegged my bivouac sheet out in the shelter of one of the dunes, and gave Half-Shandy some food and water. It was a beautiful spot for a camp. For a few minutes my mind played a panic loop that I was cut off, with no way out, and had no one else to help me. Then I thought the best option might be to scream about that. But this passed. Within an hour I began to feel surer of being stranded, and I slowly entered a deeper meditative state. The chatter of thoughts became quieter, less significant, and the surrounding view of Scolt Head began to transform. Among the marram, I began to appreciate the stiffness of individual stems, the grass's resilience to the wind, its shelter for the few insects that still crawled around in the sand. The colours of the dunes started to vary and deepen, becoming more complicated and richer. As it unlocked with sensory wonders, I understood that Scolt Head was a place where I could properly watch the dusk descend, minute by minute, for the several hours it took to go dark. In front of me the terns and geese worked their way across the water, calling out with their eerie, ghostly cries. The cattle on the distant marshes sank into shadow. Every few minutes I still felt the urge to turn away from the view – feeling I'd perhaps seen all it had to offer – but every time this happened, I forced myself to keep looking. Another few minutes passed, and more things appeared. New appreciations of how serene the water was in the landscape, like liquid sky poured into the creeks, and the layers of sound in the air as it stirred across the sea. The breaking waves on the shore became a mantra, a rhythm alongside which I began to breathe. There are, in fact, three stages of twilight before night: civil, nautical and astronomical twilight. It was mid-June, and at this time of the year the darkest it gets in Britain – being between 50° and 59° latitude – is astronomical twilight. It will never be truly night until mid-July.

When I have travelled in India, in the Middle East, or in Africa, I have been alarmed by how suddenly night falls nearer the equator. There, dusk seems to overtake the land with the speed of a giant bird's wing, and feels at odds with my Norfolk way of seeing things. Likewise, when I've been in Finland or Norway or – once – Russia at midsummer – when the sun dipped below the horizon just before midnight and was up again at four thirty – the milky glow of the sky has similarly unnerved me, like a fire's embers that can never quite be put out; you need to keep your eye on them.

I crawled into my sleeping bag and, with my head out of the bivouac, stared up at the huge starlit sky. The Milky Way was an intense stream arcing above me, crammed with all the extra sprinkling of stars Norfolk likes to put up there. Everything was clear and brilliant. There was half a moon, and along its terminator line I could see the nibbled shapes of craters and, just beyond, against the darkened half of the moon, a single spot of light where the sunlight was still catching the top of one of the lunar mountains. Half-Shandy settled next to me, accepting his place for the night, then began to lean against me. All this beach and space, and the dog was trying to push me aside to make room. Falling asleep, I began to think that with each step I took on this route I seemed to encounter a separate step that might lead me to the side – down the path of a story, an event that may or may not have happened, or a memory either I or my family may have stored up. At this rate I doubted I'd ever reach California, because although it was there, a definite spot on the horizon, it felt as though it was getting further away.

Sexy Texture

Early in the morning the tide was low enough to make the crossing back to the mainland. The water was cold and quiet, rising almost to my waist. Carrying the dog, I felt we were crossing over to discover a new land. We walked into the Holkham dunes. They were calm and grey and had a serene quality. I've spent several Midsummer Eves among these dunes, looking out to sea as the sun goes down, feeling the heat draining from the sand and the shadows rising like pools of oil. Dunes are the most secretive of all coastal landscapes; they're filled with hideaways, they feel shifting and impermanent, can only form in breezy places, can never be properly mapped, yet also have an aspect of the fortress about them, a place from where you can look out, unseen. In summer, they heat up and become fragrant with the smells of sand, warm waxy grass and the occasional sulphurous smell of a natterjack toad. The breeze rises through them in seductive breaths. They feel intimate and private, and for this they also feel sexy. In my early teens I went for several holidays to North Devon, and would walk inland off Woolacombe or Croyde beaches to wander among the dunes. The vast sound of the sea – with its noise-layers of waves and people and holidaying – would vanish among the hushed slopes. The sand would burn my feet where it was roasting in the sun, yet where it was shady there was still a night-time coolness. Among the dunes there would be lads – older than me – lying down in the sun with girls languishing on towels listening to Sony Walkmans or, occasionally, couples lying on top of each other, negotiating swimsuits, giggling and glancing at me as I stumbled across them. Sex and dunes, dunes and sex; whoopee-doopy-do.

I once slept the night in Death Valley, California, and just after sunrise I drove to an area of pure white sand dunes I'd seen from the road the day before, in Mesquite Flat. When I parked the car it was still early, and I walked among the dunes in total silence under a shimmering sky. In the distance, the rocky flanks of the Panamint Range rose up in a continuous craggy wall. Red ants scurried across the ground, and flame-coloured dragonflies buzzed past, looking like they were made of wire and tin foil. I left a line of footprints across the pristine sand, lost myself in a trance of peace and tranquillity, and gently cooked myself as the sun rose, not really realising just how hot it had become. The sun fixed itself in the sky like an acetylene torch. When I eventually returned to my car I didn't recognise myself in the mirror: red-faced, sweating, with a flicker of desert madness in the eyes.

I realised in that moment that deserts were perhaps a bad idea for me, and furthermore, my experience in Death Valley was similar to several other incidents where I nearly lost myself in deserts: such as wandering off the track in the Wilderness of Zin in Southern Israel, entering a snakelike labyrinth of wadis and cliffs, totally unaware of where I was; or the moment at the southern end of the Dead Sea, where I'd managed to lose myself among the crystal sharp ridges of sand looking for Lot's pillar of salt. There was something about deserts that was drawing me into them, into their emptiness, their sense of vacuum, their absence. One day I'd go too far, and might not come back.

Beyond Holkham's dunes are banks of fir trees, where in summer the warm beach air drifts between the trunks, picking up the resinous scent of sap and pinecones. The boughs creak gently. It's a seductive, fairy-tale landscape. Lie down, the air tells you; your journey needs a rest, lie on the soft grass and let petals fall on you. Close your eyes now, close them, and when you wake you might see the object of your desires wandering among the glades. There! Among the shadows! A glimpse of a dress, of long hair dappled with sunlight...

Yes, Holkham woods invites this kind of sensual reverie. It's a sexualised landscape, full of sexy-texture. A sensory overload of soft sand and rough bark, of spiky grass and gentle breeze, sharp salt and warm sap.

It's not surprising, given its remoteness, that a stretch of Holkham beach (marked off between two signposts) is set aside for nudists. But because this is a windy and desolate North Sea coast, it's not quite as enticing as it might sound. Once, in my mid-twenties, I went there with a girl, and we sat on the hard shore with our clothes off, being stung by gritty sand blowing along the beach, while two or three naked men sat near us. It was an oddly bleak experience, and strangely liberating in the way that being drunk in front of your parents is also vaguely liberating, albeit mixed with a dose of humiliation. While we sat there with our bums on the damp hard sand, a retired couple wheeled their bikes along the shore, laden with camping gear. They leant their bikes together in a well-practised way, calmly got undressed, then piled their clothes onto their shoes to keep them off the sand. Not much was said, and they sat down next to each other, looking out to sea. His back was leathery and sun-blemished, and she was more tanned and thinner than she'd seemed in her clothes. I remember this couple distinctly, with significance, and have often thought they taught me something about a future life I should aspire to. They seemed entirely free and unhindered, and the kind of couple so at ease with themselves that talking and observing and discussing had clearly become less important than just being.

I thought about them, again, as I walked past the signs for the nudist colony, and wondered where that couple was, now. I hoped the man was bringing his wife an early morning cup of tea, with a round of toast and a pot of her favourite marmalade on the side.

No one was about, and the beach looked hard and punishing. The scale is vast here – at low tide there can be a mile of sand to cross before reaching the sea – and there is an exoticism, too: things seem to wash up at Holkham that are not found on other stretches of Norfolk's coast. High tide lines of razor clam shells, washed up by the million, tinkle like wind chimes in the breeze. They look like the fake fingernails that litter the pavement outside South London nail salons. As I walked this glittering line with Half-Shandy, we came across the partially buried corpse of a dead seal. Amid its wind-blackened skin I could see a line of teeth and, further along its body, a section of spine breaking through. At first sight I thought about the merman who was caught in fishermen's nets off Orford Ness, in Suffolk, during the 12th century. Fishermen, straining to land their catch, had gazed down into the water and seen the face of a man looking up at them, quietly at peace in the murky grey of the North Sea. It's an odd story, even for East Anglia. They hauled him into their boat, where he lay gasping among the rest of the catch. They didn't know what to do with him, and the fish-man spoke no words, so they handed him over to the authorities who immediately put him in leg irons and imprisoned him in Orford Castle. Suspecting he was some kind of demon, they inspected him, and discovered webs between his fingers and toes, and underneath his hair were the remnants of fish-scales. They repeatedly tortured him, trying to make him speak, but he remained mute. When they offered him food, he squeezed out all the moisture before eating it. Eventually, seeing his despair and longing for the sea, his guards allowed him to swim in the Alde estuary, after tying a restraining rope to his ankle. He swam magnificently, dazzling the onlookers, then quickly escaped his handlers and the three nets they'd placed to contain him. For a further two months he remained in the estuary, a little way off the harbour, watching the village, before one day disappearing and never being seen again.

In October 2016, a forty-two-foot fin whale was washed up here, between Holkham and Scolt Head. The fin whale is the world's second largest animal, can dive a thousand metres, and outpace an ocean liner. It's also very rare, is on the endangered list, and almost unheard of in the North Sea. I was in London at the time, and when I saw the pictures on the Internet I felt something of what Albrecht Dürer must have felt when he heard reports of the Zeeland whale in 1520. Three days later, I drove up to Norfolk, not knowing whether the tide would allow me to reach it, or whether the zealous North Norfolk Council would beat me to it with their truck load of explosives. I took a torch, fully expecting to wade out into the water to see it close up, after dark. This feeling of doubt and apprehension lasted all day, until the moment I stood on the Holkham dunes as the sun was going down, and saw the whale on the far off sand.

I crossed the beach and, despite the wind and volume of air, began to smell the whale from a few hundred feet away. An autopsy had taken place. Its guts were loose on the sand, and its body had collapsed a little, but it was still a magnificent sight. I touched it below the lower jaw, on skin that was perfectly smooth. Its mouth was huge, easily able to fit a whole family in it, and its tongue – which was as big as a sofa – trembled slightly in the wind, giving an eerie impression that the whale was still alive and about to speak. A row of stiff baleen plates was clearly visible beneath the upper jaw, like the strings of a grand piano, and its throat was lined with beautifully deep grooves; all of them perfectly parallel, sweeping down towards its belly. In contrast, the top of its head was black and rubberised, like a giant aubergine, but sculpted into the streamlined shape of a speedboat. I realised this animal was fast, its body sleek and swept back. Its one visible eye had been removed as part of the autopsy, in a crude star-shaped incision as if it had been done by a pastry cutter. I put my hand on the skin by its twin blowholes, and felt the body give a little when I pushed. It was all mouth and head, but didn't really have a face, so it was hard to identify with. I thought of its life, diving a thousand metres down into the darkness. Of it sleeping out in the ocean, or socialising in pods, that even something this size had a mother and father. That it had seen incredible things. And I thought of its dying, getting weaker in the North Sea. How it would begin to give into the waves and tides until it felt the soft shelf of the sandy beach beneath it, and knew that the beach was support and death in equal measure.

It strikes me now that our connection with the landscapes we know is constantly being redefined. At Brancaster, I will always feel the absence of the sperm whale, and at Holkham, as I walked across the beach where the fin whale had been, it too had become a loaded place, defined by what had once been there.

On the hard sand the dog bolted off, stretching his legs and arching his back at top speed. He ran ahead, yapping with excitement, and stopped at a roped-off area next to the estuary. When I caught up with him, I saw that within the enclosure there were a couple of seals lying by the channel, both of them looking like rolls of carpet that had been fly-tipped there. The roped-off area had been erected around them to keep people away, but it made the seals look like victims in a crime scene. Limbless torsos, dumped on the high tide line.

We carried on walking across Holkham Gap towards a thin parapet of dunes. The tide doesn't rise in a smooth line at Holkham; instead it curves and floods as it creeps up the Wells channel, filling the hollows of the beach and cutting the dunes off from behind. There, Half-Shandy and I sat among the soft sand, looking out across a landscape of beach and mud flats that appeared to stretch forever. A couple of miles away the sea looked like a line of static in the rising heat haze. Distances were clearly deceptive, and the flattened landscape seemed to be made from colourful bands of brown sugar, golden caster and rich muscovado. In front of us, the Wells channel was filling with water and – like all estuary mouths – seemed to flow in and out at the same time. A line of surf was breaking over a small sandbank, then suddenly the bank submerged and the water became calm above it, hiding what lay beneath. The water flooded in, creeping across the beach in a soft foam. I felt I was in the middle of the great expanse of flow, of currents of air and water. And I felt brim-full with it.

Time Travelling

I left Holkham beach, passed the *wash and wag* self-service dog washing tub in the car park, then walked into the town of Wells-next-the-Sea, where I felt a sense of achievement that Half-Shandy and I had spent the night on an island off the coast, under the stars, while everyone we saw had spent nights in their own beds. I felt free and unhindered, part of a natural planet, living a memorable day rather than an unremarkable one. The day before I'd been on Brancaster Beach, looking for the place where the sperm whale had once been, but that moment was now in a queue of so many other sensory experiences – of the night on Scolt Head, the waves in the moonlight, the hard sand beneath feet, the dunes' silent hush, the creaking of Holkham trees – that yesterday felt like another year.

I often feel this elasticity of time when I'm outdoors, where intense solitude seems to make the clock run backwards. I once hired a car and drove to Assynt, in north west Scotland, with the intention of climbing the most beautiful and haunting mountain in the world: Suilven. Staying in a B&B in Lochinver, I drove to Inverkirkaig first thing after breakfast, then set out towards the Kirkaig Falls and the mountain beyond. I walked all day, crossing the boggy moors and outcrops of bare gneiss – some of the oldest rocks in the world – to Suilven, as it loomed up before me in symmetrical beauty, a glacier-carved *nunatak* that the old Viking traders named 'The Pillar.' For me it resembled the head of a sperm whale, made of Torridonian sandstone, facing the Atlantic. I navigated carefully that day but – on the way back – still managed to lose myself in the complicated ripples of gullies that spread west from the mountain. It was November, and as the dusk fell around me

I was scrambling through a rock gulch. Twisting my ankle there would have meant a frosty night outdoors. I found a fence that led through the bracken, and followed it back towards the road. I didn't see a single other person. But perhaps the most startling sight from that day was seeing my hire car when I finally returned to it, parked on the verge where I'd left it that morning: the car looked alien, because I had changed. I'd only been away a few hours, but it felt like years. Time was elastic, bending around me.

Now, walking into Wells, I experienced some of that same feeling: that it's possible to live several days each day, if we want to. I toyed with the idea of going to K's Burger Bar, on the quayside, because with its American-styled interior, its tribute wall to Elvis, and its signs for Route 66, it would be on-theme for my New York to California journey. Heath would have chosen the diner, I'm sure, because he likes that kind of kitsch irony, but for me the jukebox playing Gene Pitney was just a little too up-tempo for that time in the morning, and a life-sized mannequin of a girl on roller-skates with exaggeratedly long legs, holding an advertising board for *Panini, filled rolls and cakes* felt oddly confrontational.

I settled for a café nearby, and was surprised by how exotic it seemed after a night spent on the island. I looked at the salt and pepper sachets in a sharp-rimmed metal bowl, the laminated menu in a black plastic folder, and the bell above the door that rang but somehow didn't quite connect with the door when it opened. I felt a bit like David Bowie's character in *The Man who Fell to Earth*, unable to entirely grasp the signs and rules around me.

The tea was served in the kind of squat aluminium pot that's familiar right across Britain. It's a pot that should perhaps never have been designed, because there's no way the lid can be lifted without burning your fingers and, when it pours, the spout dribbles whether you take it fast or slow. When I took a sip, there was a lingering smell and taste of the dishwasher from the cup. The tea was too hot, and tasted of the aluminium pot, and of the soapy cup. The table top was waxed pine, and had a surface that would always be slightly sticky. The chairs had a wicker seat, but their backs were solid wood and they were too high, and the one I sat on was fundamentally uncomfortable. It made me sit too upright, as if I was being told not to slouch. I slid the chair forward, then to the side, under a table that was slightly on the small side in a café where – I noticed now – there was too much furniture. By my feet was a square of space too small for my bag. My jacket hung off the back of the chair, because there were no hangers. Through the door I saw Half-Shandy, his lead tied to a ring bolt, sitting in the sun and wincing in the light, and I wondered why I was putting myself through all this discomfort, whereas the dog seemed to be far better off.

I browsed through various pamphlets advertising local attractions – for Binham Priory and seal trips and, oddly, alpaca trekking on the saltmarsh. That particular pamphlet had a photo of a creature that looked halfway between a goat and a silent movie starlet, with big eyes and a Mae West expression. The slogan was: '*Meet Machu – he's the boss.*' Above the pamphlets was a sign that read: *You don't have to be mad to work here... but it helps!* I looked around for its sister-sign – the one that says: *Don't ask for credit... as refusal often offends*, because these slogans tend to occur together; slogans that hide meanness behind humour as thin as their own lamination. I began to suspect that this café was not merely a good example of how a café can get it wrong, but, perhaps, a perfect one. On the counter were flapjacks and teacakes and scones and walnut cakes, all vaguely indistinguishable. There was blandness everywhere, and poorly chosen design. Everything about the café should not just annoy me, but *annoy the hell out of me*, and yet oddly – and here's the point of the rant – in this place I felt curiously at home. David Bowie's character in *The Man Who Fell to Earth* squinted at me from the other side of the table, where he sat on his own high-backed wicker chair, failing to understand why I should like it in there. *I don't understand*, he said, in that quiet London accent that is restrained and nice to listen to and a bit too polite. He stared at me with one blue and one brown eye. He's way too thin, I thought. He hadn't touched his tea. I know you don't like it here, David, I began, but this place has something. These places are reliable. Their ordinariness is a constant in a changing world. They are places time forgot, where you can be surrounded by a benign Englishness that you understand because it's in your pores. You can hide in them and not exist for a while.

I left my soapy tea and ordered a coffee – which is the kind of behaviour that might get talked about all day at a cafe like this. *Remember that man this morning – he go and order a pot of tea, then he takes this sip and then he go and order a coffee?* Followed by a raised eyebrow to suggest there's weirdness around. Through the window I looked towards the quayside over the road and there, saw another loaded space for me: a Dutch sailing barge called the *Albatros*. The *Albatros* was the last of the sail-powered traders that plied agricultural goods between here and the coast of Holland. In 1996 I asked its Dutch skipper, Ton Brouwer, whether I could work my passage to Rotterdam and back. A few days later he phoned me and said he'd thought about it and yes, I could go and crew for him, and right at that moment – I was up a ladder decorating my living room in London when he'd rung – I suddenly had a powerful image of falling off that boat and drowning in the middle of the North Sea. It was such a strong image that, momentarily, my half-decorated living room felt full of cold choppy seawater, and my stepladder had changed into some fragile piece of sinking ship's rail that wasn't going to save me. I felt spooked. So while he was still on the phone, I turned him down, feeling instantly relieved, and yet some part of me has always regretted my lack of bravery back then. Being young is about collecting these formative experiences, and working my passage across the North Sea on a sailing barge would have been one of these. So now, looking across at the *Albatros*, it has a resonance of disappointment. But not total disappointment, because I still remember that image of the drowning, and when I look at that patch of quayside, it is also a spot where I might have stepped off dry land for the very last time, if my premonition had been correct.

Wanting to re-associate myself with this moment of *what if*, I crossed the car park and stepped onto the *Albatros*, which is now a floating café serving Dutch pancakes. I climbed down into the hold and found myself in a windowless room with maritime charts of the North Sea papered to the walls. Someone was in the galley kitchen, talking very quickly, and when he emerged I saw he was a lad of about twenty, who couldn't keep still and tended to answer his own questions. He spoke at a rate of about a thousand words a minute. There seemed to be a tinge of madness lurking in this ship, after all.

Up on deck I saw a glimpse into the wheelhouse and saw the Dutchman himself, old Ton Brouwer, sitting on a chair with his feet up. He looked at me and I glanced down, avoiding his gaze. I noticed a section of the deck where – in a parallel universe – I might have lost my footing after turning my ankle on a loose coil of rope, before falling overboard somewhere off the coast of Holland. And this man – this Dutchman whom I once let down and couldn't admit the reasons why – in the parallel universe he was the last person I ever saw, as he yelled out from the wheelhouse:

'Stupid lad! You'll be drowned by the time I turn this thing around!'

Half-Shandy and I started walking towards Stiffkey on the marsh, where we immediately encountered a peculiar sight. Coming our way were a group of people walking in single file, who appeared to be carrying some sort of low hedge between them. As they got nearer, I realised the hedge was a woollen one, and was made up of animals walking on stilt-like legs, with long necks sticking up like bathroom loofahs. So these were the alpacas, coming back from their 'trek' on the saltmarshes.

Half-Shandy eyed them curiously, perhaps not quite understanding whether they were dogs or sheep or goats, and possibly (like me) wondering how all these odd bits of anatomy – huge glassy eyes, long necks, straight backs, low bodies, stumpy tails – could be connected in one animal. It seemed you could only tell where one animal started and the next one ended because the wool changed colour – from brown to white or beige – or there was a neck and head sticking up to mark the join. Half-Shandy lay on the ground when they passed. He didn't growl or bark, but just stared at them because his world had just been redefined and he needed to lie down to think about it.

The alpacas wandered off, looking like badly made pantomime animals, perfectly at ease in this strange saltmarsh landscape. They left behind a smell of damp wool and goat. I decided to follow them, and was soon enjoying the sight of the low woollen hedge walking up through Wells high street, where their hooves slipped and clopped on the tarmac and the cars pulled over to watch them pass. Oversized animals walking up a high street is always mad. They assert their own rhythm and often their own agenda, and everyday life has to bend around them. When I was a child the circus came to Norwich, and my brother and I went down to Earlham Road to see the elephants arrive. They walked through the city towards the circus tent, then lumbered up Earlham Road pausing to look at the trees and the shops and for a moment it looked like Norfolk had gone properly crazy, with great African elephants walking past the garden fences and bus stops, flicking their tails and stopping the traffic. Out of their dry, creased bums fell soft crumbling piles of poo, and I just stared in wonder and thought *there are elephants shitting on Earlham Road!* Elephants, of course, can do as they like. I once sat on an elephant in Udaipur, India, and was taken round the town on it. It was a twenty-eight year-old named Hathi, and to get on board the owner had to tug its ear with a boat hook until it knelt. I stood on its hind leg, which was flat on the ground, then climbed up the ropes that held the seat on its back – amazed at how solid and dense a living body could be. As it lurched into the sky I had to duck under the telephone lines that were strung across the street in a cat's cradle. The elephant set off, walking through the old town at its own pace, wandering from side to side, with the whirl of Udaipur's rickshaws and carts and bikes and scooters parting around it – its great head in front of me covered in tassels and hand-painted rangoli designs. We came across a market and the elephant pushed people aside with its trunk and demanded a piece of fruit from every stallholder. Offerings to Ganesh were gladly given. It was handed mangoes, bananas, cucumbers and bowls of grain. No one seemed to mind. Several times a coin was given to the trunk and, once, a single rupee note, which the animal passed to its handler with incredible delicacy. The elephant continued its casual ransack of the market, and there was no way it was going to be dissuaded or hurried. But what I remember most from that occasion was when the elephant stuck its trunk into the doorway of a shop and the owner gave it an entire kilo bag of white sugar. The elephant thought nothing of it – just brought the sugar bag to its mouth and swallowed the lot, paper and all. I gripped the seat, waiting for an almighty sugar rush that might hurtle this animal up the street. But nothing happened. The elephant continued its unhurried pace – trunk curling into every shop, nudging past the queues to reach the counters, and an hour later it knelt again, pulled down by the boat hook. The sugar had no effect, and as I slid down off its wide back, I wondered whether it had even known I'd been up there, all along.

The alpacas turned into their farm, and I realised I'd been led to the entrance to Wells' narrow gauge railway station, where miniature steam trains run the four miles through the fields to Walsingham. The alpacas had brought me here, and accepting that my day might get stranger and stranger if I just let it happen, I bought a return ticket. Twenty minutes later, Half-Shandy and I were sitting in an open train wagon about as wide as a chopping board, rushing through the Norfolk countryside, occasionally being whipped by a loose bit of hedgerow, into a land that seemed increasingly surreal, until we approached Walsingham: place of visions and miracles.

Visions and Miracles

It seems you can have an odd time in this part of Norfolk, if you let it happen. You can sleep out under the stars, walk across a sandblasted nudist beach where you remember a retired couple you have often wondered about, have an underwhelming cup of tea with David Bowie, then follow a walking, woollen South American hedge to a miniature railway that takes you to Walsingham where, arguably, the strangeness only just begins. Walsingham is the final stop of one of England's great pilgrimage routes and a place where, in 1061, a vision of the Virgin Mary was seen. The vision instructed the grandly named Lady Richeldis de Feverches to build a replica of the Holy Family's house in Nazareth and, a thousand years later, religion remains big business here. In a village that only has one mini-market, there is a Catholic church and chapel, an Anglican shrine, a Methodist church, an Anglican parish church, a Greek Orthodox church, as well as a Russian Orthodox one, not forgetting the retreats, hostels and study centres. Even the disused railway station has been converted – with the onion dome of a Russian church on its roof, and icons hanging in the former ticket hall.

As a result, Walsingham smells faintly of candles, and is full of a kind of religious expectancy. As I walked down the main street, I kept looking for the Virgin Mary in patches of damp on the pavement, like Leonardo da Vinci used to do when he was seeking inspiration. I called in at the Pilgrim Shop, a quaint little place with a sloping floor and low ceiling, where two or three-dozen statues of the Virgin Mary were packed onto a long shelf across the back window. Among them, I spotted a slightly smaller statue of the current Pope, Francis, marked up with a twenty quid label round his neck.

In a second room there were boxes selling sixty or so types of incense from around the world, with exotic labels such as: Christos Gold Myrrh, Carnation (Ave Maria), Orthodox Cypress Tree, Byzantium, and Frankincense Gum. They also sold cassocks, chalices, crosses, holy water, wine and communion wafers. It was a one-stop shop for religion; enough to DIY your own church start-up. Hangers with highly embroidered or plain white vestments gave it the air of a fancy dress shop. Near the door was a wall covered in crucifixes of every size and style, and the sheer number of Christs stuck there bothered me. Some were depicted in agonised postures, while others stood fixed to their crosses with arms outstretched, as if to say *don't worry, I'm above this, I know how it turns out*. Standing in front of them, the ratio of serene-Christs to pained-Christs was troubling, and to pick one off the wall would change this ratio every time, making me wonder why there are so few images of Christ smiling. Buddha is often smirking at something, and I think that's what makes him so appealing: he looks like he's just farted and got away with it.

In the Pilgrim Shop the crucifixes are hanging off a peg board behind the front door. It's the same kind of perforated hardboard that's used in the seaside souvenir shops; and the effect makes the merchandise look mass-produced. In the souvenir shops, those boards have fake boobs, fridge magnets and various 'Keep Calm And Carry On' slogans pegged to them. In Walsingham, it's multiple Christs dying on the cross. It's not impossible that all these things are made in the same factory.

In Walsingham the shelves hold votive candles; in Cromer it's sticks of rock, with heartfelt messages.

Further up the road I tied Half-Shandy to a bolt in the wall and stepped into the Anglican Shrine of Our Lady Church of Walsingham. A service was being held inside. Prayers of intercession were being read, and fifty or sixty people were kneeling with heads bowed. The service sounded solemn and dignified, and there was an overwhelming smell of incense that, combined with the warm air rising from the central heating pipes, reminded me of my years as an acolyte at the village church where I grew up.

I wandered quietly round the church before stepping into the room known as the Holy House. It was a small space, windowless, lined with the flickering of many rows of votive candles, and at one end was the statue of the Our Lady of Walsingham: a replica of the one taken to Lambeth and burnt in 1538. It's a strange statue, surrounded by golden panels radiating a sunburst design across the altar and ceiling, making it look more like a

Hindu deity than a Christian one. Also, Mary wears an oversized and heavily embroidered dress, much too large for her, like Barbie in a wedding gown, or those dolls whose dress is used to hide a toilet roll. Surprisingly, her expression was rather angry, and it was this apparent anger that gave the room a feeling of great presence. It was a statue I didn't want to turn my back on, and a chapel that was unexpectedly moving.

Walsingham had confused me. In its souvenir shops I'd found a mass-produced side to religion that has always annoyed me, with blatantly beseeching expressions on its statues and general relics that suggested a conveyor belt of Christs, somewhere, passing a quality control, where figures with missing fingers and imperfections from the moulds would presumably be dumped in a crate to be re-melted. And in the Holy House, a rather ridiculous figure that looked in-between an oversized doll and an irritated child, lost among excessively gilded patterns – but a figure that nonetheless owned the room with a palpable sense of presence and mystery. Yes, it was confusing. There, in that shrine, I'd felt religion's ability to unnerve and cause speculation, and I'd felt myself drawn to it.

I sat on the steps outside the Shirehall museum, wondering about these confusing signals, and how they would be found at the end of a pilgrimage. I've travelled along the route of the Camino de Santiago in Northern Spain, watching the pilgrims in their high-tech walking boots marching over the fields with a staff in their hands. At the cathedral in Santiago de Compostela, the tradition is to touch the scallop shell by its front door, which I did, feeling a cheat because I'd arrived there in an air-conditioned hire car, and I'd wondered whether a sense of destination being reached was ever enough. It's quite clearly the journey itself that is the true pilgrimage. And I realised, in Walsingham, that this journey across the east of England from New York to California was also a kind of pilgrimage, through the places I have known and the places my family have known. Reaching California is not important; it's the journey that matters. The start and end point are only there so we can reflect on the larger journey that is life itself.

I still felt bothered by the statue of the Virgin Mary I'd seen in the Holy House, and kept thinking of how it stared across that dark windowless room. Perhaps Walsingham was a holy place after all. Perhaps visions and miracles were still present in this part of Norfolk. I closed my eyes, waiting for some form of spiritual guidance, but the only voice I heard was that deadpan German tone of Werner Herzog again. A voiceover from a Walsingham documentary he's never in fact filmed:

Werner: (on voice-over) when I picked up the tiny plastic figure of St John the Baptist from a tray where fifty other St John the Baptists were in a pile, I was reminded of a car boot where I'd seen a job-lot of American pro-wrestler dolls in a crate, and a sense that as we move through life we are encouraged to mark it by buying these trinkets, attaching them to our life as the magpie lines its nest with pieces of tin foil. Our houses become full and we become submerged with the souvenirs of a life we are no longer living. We should be like the nomads of the Rub' al Khali, who view possessions in terms of the weight they bring, and need to live a life that holds on to nothing.'

Again, Werner goes on a bit, but you get the point.

Before we parted our ways, Heath had encouraged me to go to Walsingham. What interested him most was the annual pilgrimage through the village on the last bank holiday in May, where High-Anglican priests in fine robes lead the procession past groups of extremist protestants who hold up banners and placards and brandish black Bibles as they heckle behind picket lines. In one photo I've seen, a dark suited man holds up a black Bible in one hand, while in his other he has a handwritten placard that says:

JESUS NEVER ORDAINED SODOMITES. NEITHER SHOULD THE CHURCH!

I'm all for stirring up a bit of protest, especially in a sleepy Norfolk village, but I do wonder what the point of all that hot air actually is. I suppose it's something to do with my gang is better than yours, which seems to be the problem with religion as a whole. And Norfolk is a very religious place. It's often quoted that while Norwich has a pub for every day of the year, it also has a church for every Sunday. Any view over the Norfolk countryside tends to include the sight of not one, not two, but three church towers. A thousand medieval churches were built, and 659 of them are still standing, making it the most densely-churched area in Europe. Wherever you are in Norfolk you are never far from one of them, and I think there's something innately puritan about the people from this side of England. After all, the original pilgrim fathers that left for America on the Mayflower set off from the Boston quayside, and to this day puritanism might be seen as this region's most influential export. The East Anglians can, at times, be a strange lot, and perhaps have the residual strains of German, Dutch, Huguenot and Nordic DNA that give them a cold reserve that is not entirely English. Friendships don't always come easily here. And this is compounded by the region being notoriously isolated. There are villages where you can still happily leave your house unlocked all night, where a neighbour fixing his fence is a major event, and where the drone of a distant tractor ploughing a field can induce an almost hypnotic state. For some, isolation leads to religious fervour. For others, it's plain eccentricity that – out here – is allowed to grow unchallenged, and has enabled the phrase *Normal for Norfolk* to be used as an excuse for almost any type of behaviour. When you grow up in Norfolk, as I did, you don't really understand the term *Normal for Norfolk*. You know no different. It's only when you leave, that you cast a fresh eye on some of the things you witnessed and realise yes, that was normal, but certainly *not* normal at the same time. As an illustration, a friend of mine grew up on a farm by the River Tud, where one of the local farmers was called Mr Milk, and another was, incredibly, called Mr Teat. It didn't stop there. One of the cattle handlers working for them was called Mr Bull and – truly amazingly – another beef farmer was called Mr Rump.

Just how did those farmers manage to keep a straight face when they phoned each other? The scene goes like this:

> TEAT: (answering phone) Billy Teat.
> MILK: Hello Mr Teat, it's Mr Milk.
> TEAT: Hello my friend, what can I do for you?
> MILK: I got a cow loose in the forty acre. I reckon it's Mr Rump's but I just wanted to check it weren't yours.
> TEAT: No that ent mine. But Rump's are off at market. Could be Mr Bull's? One of Bull's bulls got down the lane last week.

Now that's not a *normal* exchange, is it?

Or take the occasion, recently, when my brother was walking past Cow Tower in Norwich, when he saw an elderly fishermen – sitting with his young grandchildren on the bank – who had just dragged a fully inflated blow-up-doll from the river. The doll, complete with a set of handcuffs round her wrists and a startled expression, was left to dry on the riverbank like a grotesque body in a murder scene, while the children played on her, bending her legs up and down, and the fisherman chuckled away as he threaded maggots on his hook.

The Pit and Point

Back on the coastal route, I walked across the Stiffkey (pronounced *Stoo-key*) saltmarshes – passing the village that had briefly been infamous for the vicar who spent his weeks 'saving' London's prostitutes, before he returned to North Norfolk to deliver his Sunday sermon. This was the man whom my grandmother saw sitting in a barrel in Skegness, before he was killed by Freddie the lion in 1937. He's buried in the Stiffkey churchyard, where three thousand people packed the village for his funeral, and down in the soil his skeleton still possibly shows the bite mark of the lion's jaw on the vertebrae of his neck.

The saltmarshes here are vast and deep. Stiffkey is where Henry Williamson, author of *Tarka the Otter*, farmed land in the 1930s. After long days in the fields he would come down to the marshes and bathe in one of the warm pools, wallowing in the silty water that feels like silk between your fingertips, waiting for the dusk to fall.

Half-Shandy and I walked along the springy dried mud of the footpath, towards the distant heat haze rising off the mudflats. Behind us, the wooded islands off Wells seemed to be levitating – like scenery drapes in a theatre that could be slid back and forth to rearrange alternative landscapes – and it made me feel that ahead of me and behind me the views were both dubious in their reliability. Above me there was the trill of skylarks, and from hidden creeks there was the eerie cry of oystercatchers, but none of these birds could be seen. Distantly, seabirds flew above the estuary mouth, flickering like tickertape dropped from a skyscraper. I've read that some of these migrating flocks can be as large as a cloud, moving fast and low against the prevailing wind and, in concentration, can be so dense they give misleading blips on military radar. This is clearly a trickster landscape with its very own idiosyncratic rules.

I quickly arrived at Morston, where a channel winds its way in from the sea to a creek lined with boats and wooden staithes. Morston is a spiritual home for me, the place I have always been drawn to because of its frontier between softly rolling Norfolk fields on one side and saltmarsh on the other. The creek is also a gateway to an open wilderness beyond, and it seems to usher in this sense of the untamed and the free. Standing on one of the old wooden staithes, with the brown water coiling round the posts of the jetty beneath me, I'm like a bee sensing the invisible stream of salty pheromones flooding in. Morston marks the outer limits of my childhood world. From here on, the coast will have a kind of super-familiarity to it: every part of it is somewhere I've cycled or walked to, beaches I've swum from, heaths and hills where I've watched the trees themselves growing up alongside me. And in the same way that my mother's childhood wanderings came to an end with the two goats marking the frontier at Anton's Gowt – there is a sentry goat at Morston too.

The goat at Morston in his sentry box, guardian of a frontier.

I've brought my children to Morston many times, and as I stood in the car park with Half-Shandy I felt their presence, knowing that my onward journey would bring memories of their childhoods too. Over there, the large pool of slick mud behind the car park where I used to wallow with my eldest son, going for a mud walk, sliding around till we were covered from head to toe. There, the snake-like creek where I've paddled with them in the canoe, their young arms reaching out to pick samphire to nibble as we pass.

As I stopped to look across the saltmarshes, I felt a great sense of homecoming. This is the landscape I truly understand. Perhaps my upbringing among the labyrinth of the saltmarshes explains why I also felt so at home in Venice in my twenties. A maze of Venice's twisting *calli* made total sense to me, and I rarely got lost, as it resembled the familiar patterns of creeks and gullies of the marsh it was built on. A small bridge over a Venetian canal was just a creek that should be jumped, and a tiny *ramo* leading down to the Giudecca or Grand Canal made me feel like I'd reached the deep water of the Morston channel and knew I had to swim. A map of Venice and a map of the Norfolk saltmarshes look uncannily similar. Both have a resemblance to the surface of the brain, full of the cerebellum's curving lobes. And wandering around Venice or among the saltmarshes has often had this feeling for me – that I was nearly lost, but finding myself, in some vast outline of a human mind.

My brother and I have always kept boats here, most of them patched up and badly repaired and roughly painted. Most notoriously a rowing boat called the *Lady Godiva*, named in rhyming slang because it cost a fiver, and *Misty*, an ugly polyurethane fishing cuddy with a cabin that looked like a garden shed, and an outboard engine that sounded like a one-man band falling down a flight of stairs. The engine was so loud, in fact, that when we took it out to see the seals one day it drove every single one of them off the island in a blind panic. The tourists moored there – taking photos of the seals with expensive cameras – looked at us with horror. We circled the island in a cloud of two-stroke exhaust fumes, rattling the sea with our engine, before heading back. And on our return to the quay the outboard exploded, forcing us to flag the tourist boat down and beg for a tow.

Oh well, we ruin many people's days when we're young. But I did love those boats. Each of them delivered a simple promise: to make you love the water. But the sea here is a complicated thing. After ten minutes of paddling down the Morston Creek from the quayside you arrive at a choppy saltwater lagoon. The wind rushes at you, the water stiffens with ripples, and your boat drifts awkwardly between tidal flows you cannot see. This is an estuary mouth called the Pit – a three-mile-long stretch of water that, at high tide, is a vast steely inlet half a mile wide. On the other side of the Pit is Blakeney Point, a natural sand spit ten miles long that curves into a fragmented collection of scimitar-shaped beaches.

The Pit is a confusing body of water. The tide floods in quickly, spinning the boats on their moorings, then rises steadily through the maze of creeks and gullies on the saltmarsh. The water seethes with an energy that makes it feel like a living thing, searching for hollows and cracks to creep into. Then at high tide, the water seems to tremble with the effort of keeping an equilibrium. The loose grasses and seaweed float idly, and the bright green samphire that grows along the sides of the creeks stands half-submerged. The balance of energy feels tense and expectant, then suddenly there is a shift and the outflow begins – not smoothly – but in surges. The water slides unevenly across the seabed, becoming a giant twisted ribbon of fast and slow currents, pulling out to sea.

Landing on Blakeney Point always feels like stepping onto an undiscovered country. I go there as often as I can, swimming across in summer and paddling across in winter, when it can be so cold that remnants of ice cling to rim of the canoe. Among the dunes and marshes, there are wrecks of boats, eroded down to their rib cage hulls, revealing skeletal wheelhouses and rusted engine blocks that look like they're made of granite. The iron sheeting bends in the wind and the paint on them has the blistered look of psoriasis.

Underfoot, Blakeney Point feels like solid ground, but its mixed banks of sand, shingle and mud have been working their way along the coast for centuries, continually sculpted by waves so that, really, it could almost be considered a thickened version of the sea itself. Its sand bars and gravel banks curve in a sinuous imitation of the currents that formed them, and although the marram and saltmarsh plants have put down roots, it's almost as if they're rafting on a slowly flowing liquid land. Every so often a sandbar will roll away in its entirety, as happened in 2016, revealing the wreck of the 976-ton SS Hjordis, which had sunk exactly one hundred years before, fully laden with coal. Apparently the fires burned hot in the local hearths all that winter, before Blakeney's sands rolled over it to hide it from view.

I came here once in November and, after crossing the marsh, stumbled into the pupping areas of the grey seal colony. Among the hollows and sand drifts there were twenty or so pups, lying on their sides, covered in downy soft hair. Some of their fur had already moulted, and it had blown among the surrounding grasses like a soft cloud that couldn't quite be focused on. They watched me with their sad onyx eyes and, when I stepped too near, they suddenly transformed, letting out snarling coughs that sent me away. These limbless seal pups fascinated me. They seemed abandoned and vulnerable, and in the couple of weeks they'd been alive had known only the patch of marram around them. They'd be there in the middle of the night, alone under the stars. What did they know of the world in this short time? How could they look so pleading from six feet away, and so vicious at one step closer?

Perhaps they know that they are born on an edge, and that due north there is nothing until the ice pack above Jan Mayen or Svalbard. They lie on one edge of the sea, and in a certain direction the next mammal from them is a polar bear.

So Blakeney Point doesn't really feel like land and it doesn't feel like sea. Instead it seems to belong to a third category – a kind of marine foothold that shares aspects of land and sea, but is its own thing: a permeable frontier. Much of North Norfolk is like this, and it's one of the reasons why I chose to write about this area in my first novel. I wanted to put my characters here, on this liminal salty border, and see how the landscape might bend them. In my late 20s and early 30s I reimagined this place, overlaying it with a fictional life which made it exotic and intricate, and although all that writing is a long way behind me now, it stays with me nonetheless and is present each time I come back.

I pressed on along the raised flood bank to the village of Blakeney, where I sat in a caravan by the quayside and ate three oysters alongside a portion of chips served on a Styrofoam tray. It's a regular caravan, still with its cupboards and pull-out beds, but doubles up as a makeshift café. Through the window I saw a framed view of an English coastal village: kids along the quayside crabbing with lines and buckets, an ice cream van, expensive cars parked on the gravel. It looked gentle and benign. I think I prefer this place in winter, when the wind is out to get you, and the sky has the look of cut flint.

After the oysters – which were a little tasteless – I went to a shed next door that serves as an art gallery for local paintings. Frames covered the walls from floor to ceiling in a pell-mell of sizes. The subject matter tended to be quaint or nostalgic: sunsets, fishermen's boats, churches. Most of the paintings had a light that was too brightly uniform and not something I associate with Norfolk. There were flint barns with wonky roofs, farm gates hanging on the slant, and churches set in front of dramatic skyscapes where the sun was practically exploding through the clouds with a kind of nuclear vigour. There were boats and windmills. More sunsets. But no pictures of Budgen's car park in the drizzle, or a Nissan car showroom on the outskirts of Cromer, or a bus stop in Sheringham next to Poundland. Where were the paintings of workers in hi-vis re-gravelling the shore defences at Cley, in dreary February light? Or the multitudinous random splendour of a car boot in the rain, where the piles of abandoned dolls and action heroes lie on the tarpaulins like mass graves in lurid Technicolor? Why were there portraits of craggy fishermen but not portraits of the Tesco shop assistants, the estate agents, the insurance brokers, the overburdened teachers? Clearly, art is there for escape, but I wondered about these sugary views and couldn't help thinking they were only a very limited slice of what it's like to be from Norfolk, and to live in Norfolk, and to understand Norfolk.

Kippers for Energy!

Cley has a famous windmill that presides over the reed beds like a lighthouse. It has cottages built of knapped flint and soft weathered bricks, is quintessentially charming, and is a tourist jewel in Norfolk's coastal tiara. It is well known for having a smokehouse, and that smokehouse is well known for having a papier mâché man on display, holding up a beach towel behind his back emblazoned with the slogan: KIPPERS FOR ENERGY!

I understand why this man is here. It's a smokehouse selling kippers, after all. But when I walked into the shop I noticed two other figures had joined him. A papier mâché fishmonger on one side, and a woman in some sort of

S&M outfit on the other. They made a strange tableau among the pots of pâté and prepared crab. The kipper man used to stand in the window, where he happily flashed the passing cars. There he was a free spirit, so full of his own omega 3 that he virtually glowed with life. But now he was in the fridge and it seemed a bizarre ménage à trois was going down. I casually asked the man behind the counter what the story was, and was told the Kipper Man belonged to the former owner of the smokehouse, and that the particularly voluptuous S&M woman was modelled on his wife. The winter nights are long in Cley, so anything is possible, and I imagined the crack of a dominatrix' whip in the darkness. Where was the former owner now, I thought? Tied to a table perhaps. Then I decided not to worry too much. Perhaps more would become clear when the next figure turned up in the cabinet. I bought a tub of bloater pâté instead, a crusty roll, and a crab.

Halfway down the street I stopped at the house where – around the windows, below the roof, and surrounding each panel of knapped flint, there are borders made up of vertebrae stuck into the cement. It's called Whalebone House, but I think it's likely those hundreds of bones come from seals. The smell of smoked fish drifted around me, and I reminded myself that in the churchyard some of the old tombstones have skulls and crossbones carved into them. This village belongs to the sea. Many of the graves are for drowned sailors, and at the ends of the church pews, the carved figures look like a type of local fish-human. Perhaps the merman of Orford had come from Cley, where there'd once been an entire congregation of webbed-footed fish people?

Cley-next-the-Sea, to give the village its full name, is very much on the edge of the land, and the sea has sometimes come knocking, most notably in the great flood of 1953, when the tide rose up to the chimney pots and Lonnie Lemon's haystack was seen floating, intact, across the marsh in the distance. When the flood receded, a high tide of dead rats girdled the entire village. I wrote about this flood hitting Cley in my first novel, *Salt*, and it's a passage I have often read out in bookshops and at literary festivals and, once, on radio in New York, where I deliberately changed my English pronunciation of a buoy from '*boy*' to the American '*boo-ee*,' because otherwise they would think a kid was floating up the street clanging on the doors in the middle of the storm.

As Half-Shandy and I approached the windmill, those scenes of frightened people escaping the flood by smashing through their roof tiles seemed a long way away. Now, Cley is painted in hues of Farrow and Ball and the houses and cottages look immaculate and a little bit like they belong to another planet. A heritage planet, which is all about keeping a quality of the past, but entirely ignoring it at the same time. Live in a reed cutter's cottage, but know nothing about reed cutting. In Cley you don't buy your milk in a corner shop or post office, you buy it in a delicatessen where it's displayed alongside artichoke hearts and quinoa salad with edamame. The other shops in Cley are art galleries where, as you hop into the doorway to let a car pass, you hear a snippet of classical music and smell dried flowers set on the windowsill in a delicately glazed porcelain bowl. Next to the bowl might be a curious curve of driftwood or a whimsical seagull standing on a wooden perch, painted in primary colours and with an eye that looks nothing like the cruel sea-eyes of a herring gull. In the street outside, the cars begin to edge themselves between the buildings. Over the years cars have become bigger and bulkier, and Cley's high street is no longer wide enough for a Lexus RX to pass a BMW X6. As a result, it can turn into an antagonistic traffic jam, with weekending families facing each other off from behind expensive windscreens, waiting for the lesser family to back down. Cley has always been a perilous place that attracts a flood, but now it's the flood of visitors – attracted to peace and quiet – that often destroys the very essence that brought them here in the first place.

Half-Shandy and I walked down to the shore, where the beach road ends in the gravel car park nestled behind the flood bank. This was where the most eccentric café in Norfolk used to be. It was a wooden shack that looked a bit like a watchtower and a lot like a garden shed, with a heavy door that needed a strong shove to get inside. In winter, after the coastal wind scoured you to the bone, you stepped into a tropically moist fug as thick as in the Palm House at Kew. People's glasses would steam up instantly, and when they wiped them clean they saw perma-damp tables and chairs, and leaflets and posters on the walls all curled up and useless. Everyone sat in a kind of stupor, first stunned by a wind that had knocked them about, then confused to find themselves sitting inside some kind of sweat lodge. You would strip down to a T-shirt, wipe the condensation off the window, and stare out at a duck by a puddle in the car park, being so battered by the wind it was nearly reaching tipping point. A famous logbook was open on the counter, with the daily bird sightings recorded in a baffling series of codes, such as *pectoral sandpiper, North Scrape, 4pm* or *Pomarine skua (dark phase), Pat's Pool*. Each entry tended to have a little circular scribble next to it, where the bird spotters had tried to get the Bic working on the damp paper.

Occasionally some local wag would get subversive, writing something like: *Vultures seen in squadron manoeuvres over Glaven*, or *Pterodactyls, mating in Marsham's Creek!*, and I must admit I have been one of these troublemaking scribblers in my time. The amorous pterodactyls were one of my sightings, and a couple of months after I scribbled that in the bird book a very po-faced comment was written next to it demanding: '*Whoever wrote this, please respect that this book is for birders and naturalists to share information among their community*.' Well, what can you say? The irony being that it was true, I *did* once see two pterodactyls mating in Marsham's Creek (and as far as dinosaur sex goes, I can tell you there wasn't much love involved).

The Cley Nature Reserve is world famous as a nesting site, and you feel coerced into obeying its litany of rules and signs. Keep your dog on a lead. Drop no litter. Make no noise. Light no fires. Don't let a fart slip. Ignore these rules and you run the risk of instant disapproval. If you walk along one of the footpaths to the hides you must do it calmly, not to disturb the wildlife and, once inside the dark wooden hide, you feel obliged to hold your breath. A slot in the wood gives a letterbox-shaped view of a marsh pool outside, with birds from all over Europe milling this way and that. The twitchers watch in a sort of religious trance, but all I can ever think is that for the birds themselves this part of the Norfolk coast is their Magaluf, Benidorm and Ayia

Napa rolled into one. They're here in their thousands, living it large, wanting to get laid. *'Cley rhymes with par-tay,'* is what the geese say, where you strut your new feathers and pretend you look nothing like the rest of the flock. Let's get down 'n' dirty in the creeks! What happens in Cley stays in Cley. And as for those twitchers, ogling all that bird sex through the cool optics of finely engineered German binoculars – well they're just a bunch of perverts watching it all. They should be ashamed.

Twitchers in Cley, concealing erections.

As with the Anglia Motel in Fleet, Lincolnshire, the Cley Beach Café had its own out-of-this-world fridge cabinet with – as I remember – its own speciality of ever so slightly salty Bakewell tarts. Soggy pasty, super sweet icing; I loved that café. It had a post-apocalyptic quality where you sat among a fellow group of survivors holed out against the end of the world. Captain

Scott's base at Cape Evans and Shackleton's upturned lifeboats on Elephant Island must have had something like the same biosphere. Shackleton's men chewed their penguin meat in the glow of blubber-soaked surgical bandages set in sardine tins. They drank cocktails of methylated spirits in pints of glacier water, flavoured with ginger and sugar through Antarctic blizzards; it's both a world away and not so very different from the customers in the Cley Beach Café swallowing salty Bakewells and cupping hands round mugs of hot chocolate.

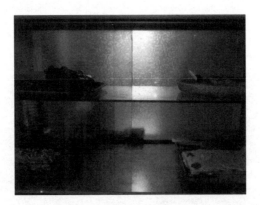

Despite so much of this journey being a coastal one, the sea is often elusive in East Anglia. Often there's a mile-wide strip of saltmarsh, or dunes, sandbars, or the four-mile length of Blakeney Point which lies along the coast like a wrecked battleship – all preventing the actual shore from being reached. The sea can be seen in glittering fragments, between the trees or dunes or beyond the saltmarsh. But going east from Cley, things change. From here on there are no more salt marshes, no more labyrinths of creeks. Here, Norfolk's coast becomes a beach, and it can be walked for forty miles to Great Yarmouth without even having to cross so much as a stream, let alone a river.

Britain's outline has the shape of a man striding towards the Atlantic, carrying a pig across his middle. Wales is the pig's head and Norfolk is the pig's arse (with the River Yare coming out at Yarmouth as an anus, to be specific). But if you view East Anglia by itself, you can also see a man's face looking down towards Holland. The back of his skull is the Wash, his eye is Dunwich, his nose is Orford Ness, his mouth is the Harwich inlet and his chin – ever so slightly bearded – is Clacton-on-the-Naze. He looks concentrated as he gazes across the North Sea towards Rotterdam, Den Haag and the outflow of the Rhine. His features have been smoothed by the sea, and he seems to have aged since his ice-age prime.

Half-Shandy and I walked east; the air was fresh and the shingle crunched under our feet. Off to our left the shore plunged into a gutsy sea, where the waves regularly crashed onto the stones, pulling and surging and building up again. Every so often a seal would surface, thirty yards or so off shore, to look at us, and I would point it out to Half-Shandy, who insisted on looking at my hand rather than the seal. A second later the seal would sink, and after half a minute or so it might reappear, further along the beach, or it might never be seen again.

On this stretch of shoreline there is nearly always a line of fishermen, each with a bivouac with the rods out front, and a thermos set into the shingle next to a bait box full of lug and rag worms. When the wind howls at them from the wave tops they sit huddled in all-weather gear, looking stoically at the rod tips and the grey swells of the sea. Occasionally a seal will look at these fishermen with come-to-bed eyes. Natural sirens, all of them. Then at night, the fishermen nestle into the bivouacs, every so often switching on small LED lamps and head torches to check their gear, so that along the shore these tiny pools of light – sometimes flashing through the orange or red sides of their windbreaks – looks like a semaphore communication between a group of men who rarely actually talk to each other.

It's a fairly brutal environment, and over the years I must admit I've never seen that many fish being caught, making me think that the reasons why these men sit out here, through the winter storms, through the miserable draughts, away from their wives, is probably more to do with disappointing home-lives than merely catching fish.

> MAN: I'm going fishing!
> WOMAN: You're always going fishing.
> MAN: I'm going fishing, coz you never put out.
> WOMAN: I never put out coz you're always going fishing.

I imagine an exchange like that has been played out many thousands of times up and down the coast. And through the night the LEDs blink out a simple multi-coloured message:

I'M LONELY. I'M DESPERATE. LOVE ME.

As Half-Shandy and I walked by I noticed some of the men were listening to radios and others were looking at mobile phones, but most were simply staring out to sea or fussing over another new combination of hook, line and bait. The outwitting of the fish, predicting their movements as they swim in and out of the off-shore gullies, reacting to flows and tides and the scent of bait, is a serious business.

Why is an exposed bank of shingle being pounded by waves something that men choose to endure and women know they don't have to? It seemed unanswerable. Not for the first time, I was struck by the similarities of spending all day as a fisherman and spending all day as a writer, and how often the process of writing a book also involves sitting patiently at a desk for hours on end, waiting for a bite on the line.

As we reached Salthouse beach, I was reminded of some friends who once came to visit me from the Czech Republic. He and his wife were in their thirties, but had never seen the sea before. So I brought them here, on a brilliantly sunny and windy day, the kind of day when all the world's air wanted to be in the same place, and I remember how my Czech friends had run up and down the beach screaming with delight at what a strange experience it was. It seemed like they'd come from outer space, landing on an alien planet, spooked when a wave rose up in front of them, then thrilled as it rushed forward onto the shore, and confused when it drained back.

From the top of the shingle bank, I looked inland towards the row of flint cottages along the coast road half a mile away. The coast road is a good place to drive alongside a hare as it races across the fields and, if you're lucky, clock it at 35mph. April hares are the best; they are even madder and lust-crazy than the March ones. My gaze lingered on Cookie's crab shack among the houses, where a thin plume of smoke was coming out from its kitchen. When you order dressed crab there, it comes served in the shell with a face made out of anchovies and olives sitting on top.

As the evening approached, and the sun began to set over the sea, Half-Shandy and I pressed on. At Kelling we came across the airfield, which is little more than a strip of mowed grass on the meadow behind the cliff top. It has a small shed and a single windsock, and one or two light aircraft ready to take off. No one was around, and two planes stood in the field, looking abandoned. This was a problem for me, because for as long as I can remember I've wanted to sneak into this airfield and steal a plane. It's just one of those irrational urges, like the sudden temptation to jump off a bridge, eat a bonnet chilli, shout out in the theatre, drop your keys down a drain, or stare at the sun. My impulse to steal a plane wasn't helped when I saw Michelangelo Antonioni's counterculture film *Zabriske Point*, which includes a sequence where Mark Frechette walks into Hawthorne Municipal Airport and casually, almost accidentally, helps himself to a plane and flies it over the Mojave desert. As I remember it, he climbs into the cockpit, starts playing around with the controls, thinks *hell, how hard can this be?* flicks a couple of switches, gets the propeller moving, guides it down the runway and up it goes. The rule of what goes up needs to be landed doesn't seem to bother him. In the film he instinctively steers his bird toward the Californian desert, where he does a dangerously low fly-pass to impress a girl who's topping up her car's radiator. He lands there, and the romance begins. *Zabriske Point* is often listed as one of the worst films of all time, but for this sequence alone it is brilliant, and worryingly compelling given my instinct to steal a plane. I had a flying lesson once, which I hoped would dissuade me from plane-theft, but during the lesson I instead discovered the secret that's never talked about: flying a plane is actually pretty easy. My instructor had his hands off the dual controls for most of the flight, looking up now and then to say 'why don't you aim for that cloud?' or 'pull up the stick till you hear a beep – that's a stalling warning – then push it down and off you go.' I was a madman at the controls, wanting to fly his rickety Cessna under Cromer Pier if I had half the chance. And I was still on the controls when we landed on the runway, when he said to me 'whatever you do don't slam one of the footbrakes, or we'll flip,' which at that moment was *exactly* what I wanted to do.

I've been to Zabriske Point in Death Valley, and I remember during the final few miles to reach it, the car's thermometer increased by a degree centigrade every thirty seconds as the road descended. By the time I reached Zabriske Point it was nearly night, and very hot.

That night, I shone the car's lights across the myriad of gullies and hills, and wandered around in the dust, walking through the same film set where all the naked couples had once made out with each other in Antonioni's film. It seemed a particularly spooky place, with an emptiness that gnaws away at your reasoning with a sense of danger. I had my hire car behind me, lit up like a spaceship, but there'd been too many people who'd travelled through this place with nothing but a canvas wagon and a billy can of stale water for it to be a neutral landscape now. Last Chance Ridge, Starvation Canyon, Badwater; the human despair was written everywhere around me on the map.

As an aside, one of those other temptations – staring at the sun – is a strange one. I've always thought we're a little too used to the fact that there's a star in our sky that will blind us if we look at it. Maybe that's why the aliens have never come to visit us – they've looked us up in the tourist brochure and it reads:

> "While the Earth is a pleasant place, not too hot, not too cold, with a range of landscapes and plentiful oceans, we do advise our travellers that it has a nearby star in its sky that, when looked directly at, will make you blind."

That's a planet I wouldn't travel to.

I managed, reluctantly, to pass the airfield without taking a plane, although I suspect the keys might have been there, under the seat, if I'd wanted. Instead, I walked towards the shore and set up the tent in a patch of heath, nestling it between the heather and gorse. The light was going, and I felt afraid of adders lurking in the grasses around me, especially the females, because their bite is strongest, so I kept Half-Shandy on a tight lead. He gulped down a lot of water and had his evening meal, then crawled into the tent with weary resignation that his life seemed to be a wandering one now, without a home to speak of.

I rolled out my sleeping bag and realised how exhausted I was. It had been a long day, and I'd nearly walked myself into the ground. I sent a couple of text messages: one to Heath, to let him know that his dog had been wonderful company, and that I was still hoping to be at Cromer Pier at 3pm tomorrow. He didn't reply. The second text was to Richard Matthews, a fisherman from my mum's village who'd promised to take me out on his crab boat. I sent him a long message explaining I was in Weybourne and could meet him at his boat in the morning, if he was going out. His reply came instantly:

7am. Bring your oilies.

I immediately regretted sending it. And I'd forgotten to tell him I had a dog with me. Oh well, I thought, too late now. I put out my torch, listening to the sea a couple of hundred feet away, and smelt the faintly coconut scent of the gorse. There's a field near here – I'm not sure which one – which is locally known as No Man's Friend, and is said to infect whomever stays too long on it with an overwhelming slough of despondency. The reason for this story is unclear, but it might be due to the belief that Weybourne's name comes from the Old English Wearg-Burna, meaning 'felon's stream,' and that this was a place where convicts were taken to be drowned in the Middle Ages. Not the nicest of thoughts to occupy yourself, when you're trying to get to sleep, and I began to wish I'd taken more care picking my spot for the night. Snakes and despondency are not good bedfellows.

As I began doze off, I thought about an aviary that used to be near here, set deep among the gorse of Kelling Heath. It had been famous for its collections of exotic pheasants, and was a place we often used to call into after my mother had hit yet another bird in her car. We would walk up to the office with a broken sparrow in our hands, hand it to them, and they would always say they'd do the best they could for it – but we never saw any of those birds again.

I collected feathers at the aviary, and would wrap sellotape round the end of a bamboo pole and stick it through the cages to pick them off the floor. Orioles and cardinals, macaws and cranes – I gathered them all. There was a mynah bird near the office, which glowered back mutely when all the local kids tried to make it say *tits* or *bumcrack*. But the bird I most remember at Kelling was an Andean Condor, that sat glumly in the corner of its small cage. The condor looked ancient, with tattered feathers and a giant beak that seemed to be carved from rock. This was the world's largest flying bird, but here it sat huddled like an old man staring into a mug of cold tea. Crouched on the floor in Norfolk, surrounded by gorse bushes and the insolent mynah bird, it looked full of psychological woe.

In a Crab Boat

I was up early, waiting on the beach in good time, and knew there might be trouble when I saw Richard's truck driving at speed across the car park, hitting every one of the puddles like it was out of control. The Toyota skidded to a halt in the gravel, reversed, then went forward again until it was almost touching the boat.

'I've got a dog with me,' I said.

'That you have.'

'Is it OK?'

'Juss get yourself ready and get in the boat. Bring your oilies?'

Another man was suddenly alongside us. He had a red face and a large beard, and he put a proprietorial hand on the side of the Toyota. He spoke to Richard, ignoring me: 'Thought you weren't never turning up!'

Nearby, another pair of fishermen, dressed in dirty yellow oilskins, were having issues with their tractor. One of them, who was bald with big ears and seemed to have no teeth, was pouring lubricant over a revolving part of the engine block. Everyone started laughing at him. Even a man operating a bulldozer repairing the flood defences started laughing at him.

I climbed onto the trailer and up into the boat and the man with the red face passed me Half-Shandy over the gunwale. 'Keep him on the lead,' he said. 'If he jump I ent going in after him.'

I stood near the prow. It was a large crab boat, filled with loose piles of poles, pot anchors, polystyrene floats, plastic flags, bright orange crates, and almost every surface covered with strands of shredded fish bait and crab shell. The paint was peeling and there were brackish pools of water under the footboards. These men didn't tie elegant bowlines and clove hitches. They just tied knot over knot until the rope stuck fast. Half-Shandy started sniffing the corners, then wrapped himself round the back of my legs.

'Here go,' Richard yelled from the beach beneath me, swinging up a grey plastic crate. 'Put it anywhere you want.' He passed me two damp cardboard boxes fastened with plastic binding. Richard leapt onto the tractor while the second man with the red face (who still hadn't been introduced) held onto the trailer, saying: 'Hold on coz that get rough down the slope.'

Without warning the crab boat began to lurch backwards down the shingle. Richard steered it fast and deliberately close to the second boat so the other men had to jump out the way. They hurled insults back at him, giving him the finger. The boat pitched at a ludicrous angle down the shingle bank, riding the shelving foreshore, then without hesitation plunged straight into the sea. I felt thrilled as the surf rose up on either side, and I didn't even notice the two men get in, or hear the engine start, or feel the boat disengaging from the trailer as it rolled and slid away from the beach.

'Wass your name?' the bearded man asked.

'Jeremy,' I replied. It sounded effeminate.

'Gary.'

The boat dipped and swayed as it motored through the water, and soon the tractor and trailer looked like a child's toy left behind on the beach. Richard and Gary started laughing because the other tractor still hadn't set off, and was belching out a cloud of thick smoke.

'Colour o' that smoke that engine's had it,' Richard said with authority, and Gary agreed, and I agreed with both of them.

They knew I'd written novels and that I was writing about a journey across East Anglia, but these things counted for something and nothing out here. Essentially I was no use on this boat. I was just a passenger. And I soon realised the layout was against me. Richard steered from the stern, and I could hardly hear him over the engine. Gary was closer, standing in a little compartment in the middle. I leant next to him, looking out at the changing colours of the sea. The weather looked highly changeable, with low, leaden clouds and squalls blowing off the land. The water was moss green close by, then it turned slate grey, then mistrustful, like mercury. Clearly I'd entered my own world because both men commented on it: 'Hope you get some inspiration out here,' Gary said.

'You best be careful,' Richard told Gary, 'see if he don't put you in one of his books.'

Gary laughed loudly, then said rather awkwardly: 'Thass all fucking and fuck and fucks-sake out here! Fuck this, fuck that and fuck the other. We don't say nothing else and he wouldn't want that in his book.'

I shrugged.

'Fuckety-fuck,' he added.

They set about the business of hauling the crab pots up. The capstan started spinning, and Richard steered towards one of his floats to hook the line from under it. The line was looped expertly three times round the capstan, until it sprang taut, and as the weight of the pots were pulled off the seabed the boat tipped alarmingly over to one side. Each pot rose swiftly through the moss green water, was lifted out, then balanced on the rail while Gary unclipped a stretchy rubber hook from the cage, swung it open, picked out anything fit for sale – which he dropped in a crate – then knocked the rest of the contents overboard. Weed and cuttlefish eggs were picked out, new bait was slipped into a noose, then the re-baited pot was swung back onto a board fixed to the side of the boat. There, it was left for a moment, like a burial at sea about to take place. Sometimes there would be a small crab left inside, or a starfish and, once, I noticed a tea-brown jellyfish stuck inside the net. Then as the boat moved, the rope sprang tight and the pot yanked forward, spinning round a metal bar to sink into the sea, holed like a colander. Gulls swooped where it sank, disappointed and frustrated.

Around Gary's boots a heap of crabs were soon jostling among themselves, their dry shells scraping, crawling for the corners, getting trodden on. There were velvet and swimming crabs among the edible ones.

I watched a velvet crab crawl up into a crafty hiding place underneath the gunwale. One of the crabs was entirely covered in barnacles – it looked like a piece of coral – and another had a giant mollusc half its own size welded to its shell. Should've picked a flint, I muttered to the mollusc, you're heading to the boiler on that saddle.

Among the crabs, I noticed miniature dramas. One of them boldly climbed across the shells of the others – using them as a makeshift ramp – until it was out of the crate and heading for an audacious escape along the engine hatch – which was a sodden piece of plywood covered by a rubber mat. Gary's attention was elsewhere, now extracting lobsters from the pots. The lobsters were bright blue and black with segmented antennae the colour of dried blood. They seemed unduly compliant with their capture, were lifeless in his hands and docile in the crate, but would then suddenly give a powerful flick of their tail to try and vault free. Gary was wise to all their tricks, and surrounded them with loose bait to keep them busy.

Meanwhile, the escapee crab nearly reached me. I was just about to flip it over the side when Gary suddenly noticed it.

'Steve McQueen he is,' he said, catching it and dropping it in the crate.

Rain swept down on us, drenching everyone. There was no shelter of any kind. All three of us turned our backs against it, and for a moment the boat seemed wetter than the sea around it. Half-Shandy cowered below me, blinking in the downpour.

'Thought you said it was going to be nothing but sunny,' I said, cheekily, a landlubber. Richard looked up at me from under the peak of his cap, taking it as a questioning of his weather-reading skills.

'Will be later.'

When the rain passed, the sea became darker than the sky, then once again took on a silvery shine while the clouds broke into black squalls. The waves picked up and rolled towards us, passing by, the sea always heading elsewhere. I watched the backs of the waves as they rolled in groups towards the shore. Every five minutes the water changed again, sometimes looking waxy as if it had a new, thicker quality, a heavier substance than it was. From a mile off, the coast looked like nothing at all – the thinnest of strips of land between sky and sea. I felt as though I'd stepped out of the frame, and was now able to view the journey I'd been on from another perspective. I saw Scolt Head, and the faint spot where I'd camped in the dunes, and next to it the fir trees and tidal islands that marked the Holkham shore. Then the bands of saltmarshes and the low scimitar shape of Blakeney Point – the land looked like a thread between the sky and sea. I was looking at a journey in itself, and it felt as though I was able to see through time, to conjure up the smell of sap in the fir woods, hear the crack of the boughs as they moved in the breeze, feel the spongy heaps of dried seaweed passing underfoot. All these sensations, present in one moment.

As we motored to the next line of crab pots, Gary lent against his hatch and told me about how much he loved woods, and how not to go under a beech tree in a storm. 'A fool's shelter they call 'em,' he said. Then he told me how much there was wrong with the terms *free range* and *organic*. And out of nowhere he said he'd been to an auction where a baby grand piano had sold for £150 pounds. Herring gulls floated by in a small murmuring crowd near the boat, downstream, riding the swells, all of them watching the fishing and Gary in particular as he dressed the pots, and cast out the old bait with delicate flicks. The gulls made a pathetic little cry deep in their throats, then rose in a busy mobbing cloud to sweep past us, diving and squabbling, fighting each other for a gulp of fish.

'What a breakfast!' I said to Gary.

'Later in the yair when them gets hungry they fight hell out of each other,' he replied.

Surprisingly, Richard joined in at that point with: 'I don't know nothing about commas and full stops.' I didn't reply – it seemed a dangerous conversation to get into, but it gave me an image of him, in an office, in a café, in a suit, in a department store – out of place anywhere that wasn't this boat. He would be lost without the sea. He started cutting fish heads in half with a long, thin, dirty knife. I touched one of the heads and felt the fish's fine row of teeth sticking proud of the jaw. A thermos of coffee was passed between Richard and Gary, but not offered to me.

A few hundred yards away the second crab boat – which must have launched without us noticing – finished tending to its pots, and began to steer towards us. As it approached, all four fishermen on both boats leant against the gunwales, like they were on a fairground ride, waiting for the piss-taking to start.

They pulled the boats alongside, hand over hand along the gunwales in rhythmic choreography, as if they were passing a rope between them, with the other fishermen assiduously ignoring me until the very last minute.

'You gonna be a fisherman then?' one of them asked.

'I don't think so.'

'You want a boat, I got the rig and trailer, boat an, all, it's all for sale. Ent no living.'

The skippers said a few words to each other, about engines and gear, and Gary said very little. There was a general feeling of complaints being shared, about the damned tractor with its lousy engine, before the boats pushed apart again, with not much else being said and little reason for them to have come together in the first place.

We headed back, and as the crab boat drove hard as a javelin towards the beach, at the very last second before we hit the shingle Gary shouted: 'Come this side!' I hurried across the boat to grab the rail just as the bow thumped into the beach. I was flung one way, then the other. This is what it's like to return to land then, I thought. It felt like I'd been in space. Gary jumped onto the shingle with a great leap and the boat lurched as each wave hit. I saw Richard hanging perilously over the stern, trying to fetch in the rudder, his legs waving in the air to counterbalance. It was a mad sight. When do I get off this thing, I thought, and in that moment I felt the land below me was full of knocks and bangs and a restless energy that I didn't understand.

Lightning and Hailstones

After packing up the tent, and a two-mile walk along the beach, I arrived at Sheringham. I reminded myself that Sheringham is a little bit dreamy and a little bit sharp at the edges. It's a town where you can watch an old person bending in the North Sea wind, their false teeth grimacing in a kind of agony, taking a full two minutes to cross the road, or a town where you'll be chased full pelt across Beeston Common by a bunch of lads because you went just a little bit crazy barging them on the summer fair dodgems, which once happened to me. Agonisingly slow, frantically fast, in the same place. On New Year's Day you can be one of two hundred people that roar charging into the sea, as if the whole world's briefly gone insane; for the rest of the year there are less exotic – but equally strange – sights, such as watching a car reversing into a parking space for a good half-hour, before it drives off, unconvinced. It's a town that feels small and big at the same time. The sprinkling of old flint cottages among a spreading street plan of pebbledash houses feels a bit like a pizza where the best bits are few and far between, on a less interesting base. It smells of chips and newsagents and cleaning fluids. And because it doesn't really have a centre, it sometimes resembles the frontier towns in an American western, where you can walk from one end of the high street to the other, vaguely suspecting there might be violence, and wondering whether you're expected to know this town for what it truly is. Are these real shop fronts, you idly wonder, or is it a stage set built for a film that never got made?

Historically, if you were born in Sheringham you tended to stay in Sheringham and, as a result, it's a town that never had many surnames. Over the years this has been a problem, especially on the fishing boats where the entire crew might be from a single family, with not only the same surname, but also – because these things get handed down – some with the same first name, too. In the days before multi-coloured waterproofs took over, these fishermen would be wearing identical dark blue fisherman's ganseys made of Worsted wool. It must have been a very confusing scene in a miserable sea fret, with the men reduced to smudges of blue in the gloom, all of them smelling very much alike and many of them answering to the same name. Not the best of situations when you're wanting a lobster pot passed to you, or when someone's about to fall overboard. Sheringham's solution was ingenious. It circumnavigated the whole official naming business, and relied on nicknames instead. The town became famous for them. In the Craske family alone there were the following fishermen: Bells Craske, Bounce

Craske, Brick Craske, Buck Craske, then: Coaches, Cock Robin, Corgi, Crib, Cutty, Dingy, Dutch, Guineas, Hanna-Gals, Helly, Jizzy, Jonah, Lux, Munchy, Ninny, Pork Pie, Sausage, Silky, Squeezer... and finally... Tads Craske.

Across the fishermen's slipway, away from the esteemed Craske family gene-pool, there were other remarkable nicknames: Tar-Wash Bishop, Sea Toad Cooper, Latter-Day Cox, Cow-Weed Farrow, Plug Emery, Pea-Cue Fields, No-Bones Gray, Butterballs Grice, Honey Grimes, Haystack Hannah, Belcher Johnson, Loose-Gas Knowles, Drips Little, Stallion Pig Middleton, Scratchums Pegg, Rook Reynolds, Greasy-Hat Scotter and Bumshee West.

From left to right, step forward: Latter-Day Cox, Rook Reynolds and Belcher Johnson.

I suppose the use of these nicknames makes sense on a crab boat, but not in many other situations, and surely has led to more of those crazy conversations that you overhear in Norfolk, similar to Messrs Teat, Bull, Rump and Milk discussing lost cattle.

BELCHER JOHNSON: Sea-Toad an' No-Bones come up the beach lookin' for Loose Gas. Only Loose Gas weren't in Greasy Hat's boat no more, coz of that business with Scratchums the other day, so they gets to Greasy Hat's and starts looking for Loose Gas and there's Scratchums already out there on Bumshee's boat all along.

The dark blue ganseys they wore held further clues to the fishermen's identities: Sheringham ganseys were famous for having a unique design of lightning and hailstones woven into them, so a body washed ashore could at least be traced to the port it came from. The gansey itself was an incredible garment. Knitted with five needles, it was made without a single seam and could be worn either way round so the elbows never wore out. Heavily patterned above the chest, for extra warmth, the weave was so fine and dense that it was both wind and waterproof, stopping short of the wrists so it wouldn't get repeatedly soaked, and had cast-off collars and cuffs so that any repairs could be performed by unravelling it from these points and knitting them out. And the true gansey's secret selling point was that it was never washed, so its knit developed an extra impermeable skin of working grease.

These impregnable jumpers were knitted by fishermen's wives in candlelit rooms, where the women would make their husbands or sons a gansey that would last a lifetime, working in images of herringbones, ropes and the weather, knitting it with love, and hoping with every click of the needles that it wouldn't be washed up on the beach one day, on the back of a drowned man.

There were six boats hauled up on Sheringham's slipway when I walked past, fixed to ring bolts on the steep cement slope. By the side of the boats were piles of chains, ropes and crab pots, but no fishermen. And not a gansey in sight. All I spotted were fleeces and breathable-outer-layered Gore-Tex jackets on the various people dotted around the seafront. A row of holidaymakers sat on a low wall, eating chips. Nearby, there was a mural on the sea wall of a man sitting in a deck chair. It looked like he was a dead man, washed up. Without his own distinctive Sheringham gansey, no one had come forward to claim him.

Just up from the seafront is a blue plaque marking the spot where the first bomb to be dropped on Britain in WWI landed, on 19th January 1915. It's a strange plaque to be found in a sleepy coastal town, and inaccurate too, because three weeks earlier there'd been a bombing raid on Dover castle, which managed to knock a man out of a tree in the nearby vicarage garden, where he'd been collecting holly ready for Christmas Day. To be pedantic, this Sheringham plaque should – instead – be marking the site where the first bomb was dropped in Britain from a *zeppelin*. That night, a couple of German naval zeppelins had crossed the North Sea, from their base in Fuhlsbüttel, trying to reach the Humber estuary, but had blown off course. Struggling to reach any kind of coast, Naval Zeppelin L4 limped over the cliffs at Sheringham, and it must have been a terrifically ominous sight for anyone out that night – for the empty sky to be blotted out by a cigar shaped aircraft as long as the town itself. Commanded by Kapitänleutnant Magnus von Platen-Hallermund, it hovered in the sky over Sheringham. A bomb was dropped, which fell through the roof of a cottage in Jordan's

Yard, passing through the bedroom and kitchen, before buying itself in the floor. It failed to explode, but landed with enough force to knock a girl off a chair. Job done, the zeppelin apparently blew out to sea again, before steering back towards the coast later that night, like a troublesome cloud, to drop a bomb in a damp field near Brancaster Staithe, before heading towards Kings Lynn.

Sheringham is probably best summed up by an event that happened there in my early twenties, when my brother and I made the questionable decision to run a pancake business from the back of my VW camper van. We parked it in the car park on the seafront one night in August, put out the banner and began to fry up the pancakes. After a while, one of the hoteliers wandered over, wondering why his restaurant was so empty of customers that evening:

'What you lads up to?' he asked.

We pointed out the pancake menu, and suspecting there was an aggressive agenda behind his question, explained how we'd got all the necessary food hygiene paperwork from the local council.

He looked at the menu for a while. Our pancakes were incredibly cheap, starting at 35p for lemon and sugar, and rising to a lofty 75p for our luxury choice of Nutella and banana. Running a business is not my metier.

'How much for everything you've got?' he asked.

We totalled it up at about six or seven quid.

'And that's everything?'

'Yes.'

'Right, I'll buy it all, thanks.'

He made us cook every one of them, watched us fold them carefully into a bag, and then, on the way back to his hotel, he dumped them all in a bin.

See: Sheringham, a little bit dreamy, a little bit sharp at the edges.

West Runton

Walking out of Sheringham along the shore, below the high grassy cliffs of Beeston Bump, I felt the magnetic pull of Runton beach ahead. West Runton is the village where I grew up and, as I approached, I began to recognise the familiar spirals of clay in the cliffs, like nougat whirls in a fondly remembered slice of cake.

This stretch of North Norfolk only has cliffs because so much earth was left here after the ice age, when Arctic glaciers moved south, pushing hills of clay, marl and gravel at a slug's pace in front of them. It was pointless bulldozing on an industrial scale, and at North Norfolk these icy shovels came to a halt, dumping several billion tonnes of earth in the process. When the glaciers melted, they left behind a series of hills with steep sided dry valleys and, here, along the coast, a battlement of crumbing cliffs constantly eroding into the sea. Sometimes it can feel as though the glaciation process never stopped, because the cliffs themselves seem like great sandy glaciers, still moving forward inch by inch into the water. Occasionally a house-sized lump of chalk will emerge from them and – over time – will launch itself like the prow of a ship as the rest of the cliffs become eaten away behind it. These ship prows nudge into the sea, as freestanding stacks that get sculpted and carved smooth by the high tides. Eventually they, too, get undercut and fall.

Impermanence makes this coast unusual: when cliffs are made from chalk, clay and sand, they age at a rate you can actually see. With each season they transform, and as they crumble into the water they have an almost human quality of frailty.

It was low tide, so I walked on the firm sand alongside the wooden sea defences. These defences are no longer repaired, and over the years their planks and posts have become dismembered by the waves, exposing long dark iron bolts – their metal now weathered as smooth as icicles. Acrylic ropes, nets and shredded plastic hang from the splinters resembling brightly coloured Buddhist prayer flags, while flints are wedged into the gaps like a pebbled mortar that's been precisely hammered there.

I looked at the cliffs with their slipways of sand where I've encouraged my children to launch themselves off the top and run and sink and tumble their way down the soft slope all the way to the beach, battling with acceleration and falling in clouds of sand. Along the cliff edge, I could see clumps of grass overhanging like badly fitted carpet, dangling in the air, ragged and threatening to fall.

Up there were the dips and hollows where I would meet girls as a teenager, sitting on the grass with the warm air rising up from the beach, while around us the cracks in the earth revealed where the cliff edge was becoming loosened from underneath. It was an appropriately precarious spot to be precarious with a girl. A footpath where I used to chase my brother, hurling sticks at him, the spot where he once tripped and broke his arm, a thicket where I used to pick blackberries, a whole rabbit warren – all of it has disappeared into thin air that lies just beyond reach, as this part of the coast successfully erases itself and, with it, seems to erase my childhood as well.

This is the beach where, for years, I rummaged among the flints looking for the blunt bullet-shapes of fossil belemnites, lodged in the chalk like broken drill-bits, where I overturned stones and found the unmistakable pinprick patterns of fossil sea urchins and heart-shaped micrasters. Perfect paperweights, every one of them. Among the banks of shingle on the high tide line, the endless walks facing the setting sun hoping the light would shine through pieces of amber among the trickster carnelian imposters. Forty years of trudging up and down that shingle, looking for that elusive Scandinavian gold, and in all those years only ever finding one piece. *A nor-easterly, and you can see the amber floating in on the storm waves*, I was told that once, and now know it was a lie I should never have listened to. But I still can't help dropping my eyes when I cross the shingle. This is the beach I walked down to every day during my adolescence, where I'd sit on the groynes and stare out to sea at the passing freighters and cargo ships. It's a place where I took some of my first photographs on an Agfamatic 110 camera, and where I still return and take photos, still fascinated by the way the light shines across the hard sand, picking out the individual flints like they are giant's teeth. This beach is where I tried to learn windsurfing, holding the sail with grim determination as I drifted over the outflow of the 1980s sewage pipe, where I capsized repeatedly in an open kayak, the waves picking me up and driving me at the shore like an arrow, where I built cairns of stones and damned the streams and waded through the banks of foam that washed up off the back of November storms, me and my brother in a grainy sea mist of spray and steam from the huge waves. It's the beach where I sat with friends and walked dogs and ate crabs and prised limpets and touched the stinging frilly centres of neon red anemones. There, among the flints, I watched a cruel mate of mine from Sheringham make a crab grasp a firework with its pincer one day. The firework was a rocket, and when it ignited the crab refused to let go, and sat instead among a blast of flames like a welder with an acetylene torch. There's the point where, one winter's evening, I was too afraid to leave the beach because I was certain the fabled ghost dog of East Anglia, Black Shuck, was lying in wait by the storm shelter. There, on the slipway, where one night in 1985, my good friend Duncan and I watched spellbound and unnerved as a meteorite exploded into a searing white ball of flame over the sea. It burned like a supernova for a whole half a second, and then vanished.

It's the beach where each one of my three sons had their first ever view of the sea. Each one, I held at the bottom of the slipway, with the water surging across the concrete apron in front of us, while their serious baby-frowns faced the North Sea, unimpressed.

By a curious twist of the coast's alignment, and in a way that is rare in Britain, at West Runton the sun both rises and sets over the sea. It never touches the land. As a child, this gave me the impression that the sun was a watery thing, wet and flooded with sealight, emerging from the sea and sinking into it every day. The sun has remained a watery phenomenon for me, ever since. A second secret of this beach is hidden at the base of the cliffs: the black line of freshwater mudstone from the Middle Pleistocene that runs from here towards Cromer, and which was once the riverbank of a tidal reach of the Rhine, or one of its grand tributaries, as it flowed north into the basin that became the North Sea. It amused me as a child that I was essentially growing up on the Rhine's riverbank, and should be able to claim a kind of technical Germanic birthright, if I wanted. With the end of a screwdriver, or the point of my geological hammer, I used to scratch and dig into this soft peaty Rhine-mud, finding frog and fish bones and fossilised wood and once, part of a mammoth's molar. Bones have been found here belonging to hyena, rhino, bears and, famously, an entire elephant – *Mammuthus trogontherii* – with a skull as large as a bus engine. It weighed ten tons and was twice the size of a modern African elephant. The skeleton was discovered by my old maths teacher. Its toe bone, when it was found, showed the tooth marks of a scavenging hyena that had attacked the animal after it had died in the river. I used to lie in bed at night, a few hundred yards away from this sleeping giant which was buried under tons of glacial deposits, imagining that this village had once reverberated to its calls, before it had staggered into a pool and died, while nearby a pack of hyenas yipped and drooled and waited their chance.

From the bottom of the slipway I could see Cromer pier in the distance. I was ahead of schedule to meet with Heath, so I climbed onto the cliff and gave Half-Shandy some biscuits and a drink of water. It had been a long day since being on the crab boat at Weybourne, and I'd hardly stopped walking. The sea was smooth and pale blue, reflecting the sky. As I sat there, I wondered why we're so drawn to the sea, and why it's rare for other animals to gaze at it the way we tend to. I've noticed dogs will happily run onto a beach and not give the sea a second glance (although Labradors do have the tendency to face the water like Easter Island statues. Perhaps it's in their bones, as well as their Labrador-name, to be a coastal dog with a coastal sensibility). But mostly, we're pretty unique among animals to stare at the sea. Its size, mystery and danger attract and humble us. It sits there, giving us a bagful of paradoxes: you can see over it but you can't see into it – it's a view of distance but not depth; its colour is any one of a thousand colours from thick gunmetal grey to brilliant azure, and yet it is always the colour of the sea; it invites you in to swim, but will drown you in an instant; it's loud and quiet; intimate and huge; planetary and personal; flat and – with a view along a horizon – also curved. Perhaps it's a puzzle that can't be solved, while attracting an idle mind to have a go nonetheless.

The North Sea is only categorised as dead calm on five or six days in every year, and only appears blue in the very height of August. For the rest of the year it's a churning muddy-grey, due to it being a shallow sea where a storm can shake up the water quicker than in most places on Earth. It can change character several times a day, can lap quietly against the beach all morning, then savage the cliffs through the afternoon. The boom of its waves can be heard several miles inland, and its salty breath makes the trees lean away in distress. In turns it's ugly, haunting, enticing, violent and seductive. And if you grow up next to it, as I did, you learn from it.

From these same cliffs I would watch, as a child, the distant freighters passing on the horizon. Their outlines slid towards each other and, as they touched, became a single lozenge shape. Like the sperm whales patrolling the coast, these freighters felt like they too were full of mystery and stories. On my early morning paper-round I would stop to lean against a gate, bracing the weight of the delivery bag on the fencepost, and gaze at the coastal freighters that had harboured close to shore. I'd wonder about the kinds of men who worked and lived on them and the kinds of spaces they inhabited. Unshaven, rough men, in oiled jackets and sweatshirts, in oversized boots, eating beans and eggs and listening to a radio, then walking off to a cabin where they'd spit or fart or watch porn or a martial arts video. Occasionally one of them would go out on deck and lean against the ship's rail and look across at the flat, silent coast a few miles away. From my place at the gatepost I would watch them. I imagined the floodlights shining over the damp steel decks, the soulless acid-bright corridors of the crew's quarters, the narrow cabin bunks with photos stuck to the plywood, the quiet hum of electricity in the wheelhouse and the frightening vibrations of the giant engine, shuddering like a beast in its own room beneath them. It wasn't hard to conjure these things, and to see in them seeds of other stories too – about the men, where they came from, the lives they would briefly lead on shore – in smoky, damp bedsits, eating fry-ups, always with one eye on the dock. Each day these stories entered my world from the east or the west, passed by, then vanished. And in their own way, these distant freighters, carrying agricultural goods north from Tilbury, or bringing machine parts south from Tyneside, were part of an education for me – a proximity to a world of stories I needed to understand.

To Cromer Pier

Three more miles, and I'd reach Cromer. The sight of its pier sticking out from the town was heartening. I'd had an exhausting walk and was ready to stop. Ready, too, after so many miles with my own thoughts, to meet up with Heath again and, as I approached, I tried to spot the colour of his jacket among the shadow of the pier's iron legs. And thinking of the crab sandwich I might have at the Rocket House café, my mouth began to water. Off the coast here is the largest chalk reef in Europe, and it's the chalk that gives the crabs their famously sweet taste. Ah – the rich flaky meat, the tang of vinegar, the soft white bread...

I know the flints along this coast so well that if I was blindfolded and shown any one of them I think I'd be able to tell you exactly where I was, just by its feel and smell. The blood red flints of West Runton, marinated in iron oxide, become the gleaming white flints of East Runton: cut them open and their flesh is obsidian black, and they have an extra high-baked ting to them when you tap them with a stone. Grind them together, and you smell gunpowder. In Cromer the flints are round and pewter grey, with pitted surfaces and many holes. In Sheringham they are fist-sized pebbles along the prom, and below Beeston Bump they are gloriously swollen and sculpted like a Henry Moore nude.

As I walked along the hard sand I followed a series of footprints made at some point that morning, and played the game of creating a character from the tracks left behind. A couple, walking closely together, within hand-holding distance of each other, his shoes having the imprint of an outdoor walking trainer, and hers a wide, flat-soled comfort shoe. A dog's tracks, weaving around them, scampering up and dashing off again, leaving orbits of marked territory around them. Then a single set of footprints veering towards the pools, going into the wet glassy sand near the sea and vanishing for a while, before coming back towards the rocks again. Another set of tracks where someone had had to accelerate and jump across a stream, a deep soggy impression on the other side suggesting they'd not entirely made it. And then a single footprint, which was eerily similar to the one Neil Armstrong left on the moon:

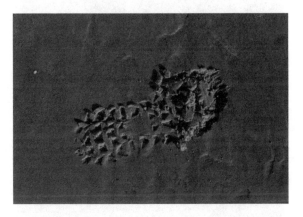

Heath was standing under the pier, just as he'd promised back in the Travelodge car park, two days earlier. It was ten past three when I walked up to him, and although he didn't mention it, I suspected that despite thirty miles of walking, sleeping out on Scolt Head, hiking through dunes, woods, saltmarshes, following alpacas, taking a pilgrimage to Walsingham, battling through more shingle banks and creeks and wanting to steal a plane, camping in a spooky field and fishing all morning on a crab boat – he felt I was letting him down by being ten minutes late.

'You look like a wild man,' he said.

'Thanks.'

On the pier, two fishermen had just caught a huge sea bass. It's the largest fish I've ever seen landed there. But rather than celebrate, they opened two cans of lager and seemed to contemplate what needed to be done next.

'All the salt air.'

Half-Shandy started scampering about, rolling in the sand by Heath's feet, overjoyed to see him. Traitor, I thought. To think how I'd looked after him, giving him regular breaks and drinks and this is all it boiled down to in the canine mind: unquestioned loyalty – you don't mess with it.

'It's good to see you again,' Heath said.

'Did you manage all you wanted to do in Cambridge?'

He shrugged. 'That's something I will never achieve. How's the dog been?'

'A very lovely companion. Didn't bite any birds. I see he's forgotten all about me now.'

'Yes. He's a rat.'

We went onto the pier and I showed Heath the theatre at the end where I once played Little Jake in *Annie Get Your Gun*, and on another occasion was one of the dirty-faced urchins in *Oliver*. The local legend is that during the hot summer performances some of the side doors to the auditorium would be left open, to allow a draught, and through these doors crabs would wander into the theatre, ushered in by mischievous fishermen. I never saw them, but like to think the story is a true one, especially as the crab – with its sideways crawl, its eyes on stalks and its raised jazz-hands pincers – is just about the ideal creature for an entrance made stage left at an end of pier show.

At the bottom of the slipway I showed Heath the tractors used for hauling the crab boats from the sea. These tractors, mostly Fordson Majors with Simms Brothers engines, have worked this beach for more than half a century. Over the decades the paintwork has blistered off, the radiator grills have become lopsided, bound now by plastic ties, and the metal seats have been nibbled away by salt and rain. The glass dials of the fuel gauges and speedometers have cracked, and the needles inside have vanished or become welded into place. From rusted dashboards the stalks of gear sticks and levers point up like the bitten-off mandibles of old lobsters. Fresh lines of welding cover the bodywork like operation scars. Tarps are draped over the engines and fixed in place with bungees and wire to keep the salt out. The tyres have no tread, and their rubber now has the ancient look of smooth basalt – it's virtually impossible to imagine that they still contain air. The engine blocks quietly drip thick oil onto the beach. These tractors are improbable, eroded, ancient, but when the fishermen climb onto the seats and turn the ignition key, the baffles start flipping at the top of the exhaust flues, the gears crunch and – incredibly – they still roar off across the sand and shingle in a cloud of diesel smoke.

My own collage of Cromer's tractors. Viewed together they are the same, and yet every one of them is unique. A different coloured tarpaulin here, a homemade exhaust there, a bungee cord like a new artery across the engine.

We went to the Rocket House café, overlooking the gangway and beach, where I happily ordered my crab sandwich.

'Did you find your oyster stone?' I asked.

'I did. Smaller than I thought, but it – like us – has made a journey over the fens to get there, so I gave it a pat on its back as a fellow traveller. The glaciers broke it off an outcrop near Sleaford and pushed it sixty miles before they dropped it off.'

'There's a lump of granite off the coast at East Runton,' I said. 'Similar story. When I was a kid one of the old boys in the village told me he remembered it sticking out of the cliff. It's a hundred yards out into the sea now. I'm surprised there's anything of Norfolk left.'

Heath drank his coffee, and helped himself to the biscuit that had been left on my saucer.

'So – where do we go from here?' he asked. 'Continue walking round the coast till we reach California? How far is that?'

'About twenty miles. How are your feet?'

'Good. These Boston trainers are doing their thing.'

'Heath – I've been thinking, I don't really fancy walking round the coast anymore. I think we need to see that other side of Norfolk – take the wet route.'

'What's the wet route?'

'The Broads. Go inland and follow the rivers to get as close as we can, then walk the last bit to California.' I took out my map and laid it out on the table – showing a possible route that would make a dog's leg through the Broads, arriving at a point five miles north of California. 'We can walk the last bit from there.'

'We'd need a boat.'

'I have a boat.'

Heath looked doubtful. 'What sort of boat?'

'I have a Canadian canoe stowed in my mum's garden at West Runton. Do you think Half-Shandy would be OK?'

'Oh, he'll be fine. We start at Wroxham?'

'No. We can start here –' I pointed out a mark on the map a couple of miles inland. 'We can put the boat in on a stretch of the Dilham canal, then go south on the River Ant as far as possible, before turning onto the River Thurne – which goes East, all the way to here.' I pointed to Horsey Water, which was a mile inland from the coast, just above California.

'What about Norwich?' he asked.

'Well, we should see Norwich,' I offered. 'Norwich was always on the direct route from New York to California. We can break the boat journey for a visit. And if we manage that then I can treat you to a lunch of brown shrimp and mushy peas at the market.'

'Sounds like a deal,' Heath stuck out his hand and we shook on it.

Beyond him, I had a glimpse of the table where my grandmother used to sit, sipping an oversized cappuccino that, in her old Welsh voice, she pronounced *cap-YOU-chee-no*, with her little finger slightly cocked to the side.

We stayed at my mother's house in West Runton that night, with Heath and Half-Shandy on a fold-out bed in the study. I sat for a while in my bedroom, wondering whether this journey had revealed what I'd hoped it would. Two thirds of the way through. Was it beginning to make sense? The fens had repeatedly felt like an area that swallowed things whole, whereas the North Norfolk coast had felt like a place that gave things back. A place where whales and giant sun fish were delivered by the sea, where storm tides unearthed fossil belemnites and micrasters and occasionally whole elephant skeletons, and where the shore itself was always being mischievous, a trickster character leaving clues along the high tide line.

I stayed up late with my mother, sharing some of my observations about the journey so far. We talked about New York and Boston, about the black dog at Fosdyke and the school building at Gedney Drove End and how she'd left the pigeon with the broken wing on the bar at Sutterton.

'I suppose they ate it,' is all she said about that particular event.

She went on to correct several details that I thought had been true. She told me she hadn't driven to Gedney Drove End for an interview, but had gone there to deliver her application for the job and, instead of driving up to the school, had decided to turn back on the outskirts of the village.

'So you never sat in your car outside the school, all dressed up for the interview?'

'No.'

'You sure?'

She laughed. 'I think I'd remember.'

It amounted to the same thing, I suggested. But my fictional version of my mother, in that moment of peril outside the school seemed so correct and strong I couldn't quite shift it. Never mind, I thought, I prefer my story with her realising our future wasn't to be in Gedney, so decided to keep it. That's what fiction's all about: a gentle extension of the truth, to arrive at a further truth.

North Norfolk, at night. Irradiated, lighting beacons for the aliens to land.

PART THREE

THE WET ROUTE

The Randy Coypu

We put the canoe in a couple of miles north of Wayford Bridge, on a swollen stream at the edge of a field. The water was full of duckweed, and overgrown with briars and bushes. Heath, sitting up front, fought with the twigs, and I could see he wasn't enjoying it. Luckily, things improved, and we were soon paddling down a water channel between trees on a stretch of river that was entirely ours. Only the occasional half-sunk boat wedged in a mooring suggested anyone had been down here before. It was good to be travelling with Heath again. I'd missed his observations, and the way he has of stopping several times each day to look at something with a slightly puzzled expression. I saw him do that in New York, at the pebbledash wall, as though he was trying to find hidden hieroglyphs. I would have liked to have seen him in Walsingham, standing in the Pilgrim gift shop surrounded by the crucifixes and saints, or hear what he thought about the papier mâché kipper man and his S&M dominatrix in Cley.

It was also good – after so many miles walking on shingle and sand – to be on a boat. When we launched it, I marvelled at how it transformed from a bulky object into being suddenly buoyant. My canoe is a dark green Old Town Canadian one, and it sits so lightly on the water that it hardly makes a dent in the surface.

After half and hour of paddling we arrived at Wayford Bridge, where the navigable system of the Broads begins. The boatyard there is a strange place. It stretches away from the river like a graveyard across a boggy field. Old wooden broads cruisers lie abandoned in long grass, propped up on empty oil barrels and covered with multi-coloured tarps, among a pell-mell of polyurethane hulls, canoes, dinghies and tenders – mostly too decrepit to float, but too cherished to be broken up, which is a lingering demise that often happens with boats. Peering through the cabin windows I could see piles of old cushions, or a kettle left on the side, remnants here and there of hand-embroidered fabric or pictures in frames; glimpses of interiors that were once cared for. It was easy to imagine the families who'd been in these cabins, inching around each other while tables were unfolded on ingenious hinges, or couches pulled out to make overnight bunks.

Among the boats, cranes and tow trucks, there were a few caravans. I looked into one and saw a toy model of the Crazy Frog staring back at me, on a shelving unit which also had some bowling trophies on it, alongside a wire skeleton cat. The room was many things – partly tidied, partly emptied, giving clues about the people who may have made it their weekend home, and I couldn't tell whether it had been last used in 2006, at the height of the Crazy Frog's fame, or last weekend.

When I took this photo, the reflection showed a blue sky that I hadn't been aware of – perfectly poised above the dining table, as if that part of the room was filled with a dreamy sense of wish-fulfilment the rest of the room was missing. I turned away from the window, feeling confused by what kind of home it represented, in exactly the same way I had once done in Alabama, when I'd stood among the entire contents of a house which had been dragged out onto a front yard. The front door of the house had been wide open. I had stopped my car to see what it meant and wandered up the path, my feet crunching on broken glass and an abandoned license plate. Inside, I discovered a room so ruined that it must have been pulled apart with real violence. Among the broken glass, torn sofas and wrecked walls there were children's toys, and a sense that this was the absolute opposite of what a family was meant to achieve together. So much of life is about creating a sense of home. But for every home that is coming together, another one is falling apart.

As we left the boatyard I recognised a cruiser belonging to one of my friends from sixth form college. It was tied to the bank with a heavy-duty lock and chain. Unlike most of the pleasure boats – often called whimsical names such as: *It's Time for Tea, April Fool, Broad Ambition, Yes Darling, Water Gem* and *Ocean's Dream* – this one was called the *Randy Coypu*, painted in camouflage decals and kept here at the yard in lieu of repairs that have never been paid for. I hadn't seen the boat for a couple of years, and was glad it was still floating – albeit impounded – and also glad there was still a sense of rebellion and counterculture out here. Some of the shacks I remember, where teenagers get high and go a little crazy, might still be found among the reeds, and half-sunk houseboats used for adolescent debauchery might still be floating at the end of silted up channels.

On the boat's prow was a graffiti outline of a coypu, giving passers by a cheeky wink. The story of the supersized Argentinian rodent – the coypu – and how it briefly ruled Norfolk, began with a three-hundred-strong jailbreak from a local fur farm in 1937, when an obliging storm knocked down a patch of galvanised steel fence. From there on, the story reads like a Pixar filmscript. The original band of escapees, who'd previously been called *swamp beavers* and were once exhibited in a freakshow in Yarmouth Easter Fair of 1935 as *giant sewer rats*, ran off from the fur farm and quickly discovered that Norfolk's reed beds, marshes, quiet riverways and sunlit broads were a kind of paradise. Unlike their British counterparts – timid water voles, dreamy field mice and melancholic rabbits – these coypus were orange-toothed, big bellied, and randy as hell. They were out to have sex, lots of it, and every nine weeks their population doubled. There were times in the late '70s when it seemed that every local newspaper and TV bulletin had to contain a mandatory coypu story, and there were more and more alarming reports of what the coypus were up to out here in the Broads. From where I was living in Norwich, we heard on Anglia Today about the rampant goings on in the reed beds, about how they were turning out new generations of delinquents that were pumped-up with muscle and running amok. There were posters in our school playgrounds, featuring animals with snarling buckteeth, which we coloured in red, alongside warnings that we MUST NOT GO NEAR A COYPU if we found one cornered. It was even rumoured – which I've since found out to be true – that the females had evolved nipples high up their sides so that their young could suckle while they swim.

CAMPAIGN AGAINST
COYPUS

This Pest Damages Crops and River Banks
IF YOU SEE ONE
PLEASE REPORT IT TO
MINISTRY OF AGRICULTURE, FISHERIES & FOOD
Southgate St., Bury St. Edmunds. Tel. 3271

So, while the rest of Britain might have been taking note of the international oil crisis, strikes, punk rock and the winter of discontent, here in Norfolk we were locking our doors, fearing the coypus would be coming for us. I imagined them gnawing their way through boats on Hickling Broad and digging up lawns just for the hell of it. Could they get through a cat flap? Could they hot-wire a motorbike? Were they riding the dodgems on Great Yarmouth's Pleasure Beach? Were they smoking cheroots in Norwich's graveyards? I've read that one was found inside a public toilet in Litchum. The fact that the toilet was locked from the inside is a mystery that still remains unsolved. It wasn't inconceivable that these same coypus were forming gangs, ransacking the Teen and Twenty Club in Wroxham, spraying graffiti on the paddle boat steamer at Horning or doing smash and grabs on the biscuit aisle at the Co-Op in Potter Heigham.

By the early '80s a full extermination programme was underway. Coypus were Argentinian, and when the Falklands war broke out in 1982, anything Argentinian was fair target for British guns. It was open season. Every few yards of riverbank had a large wire coypu trap, and a price was put on each tail handed in. Hundreds of thousands were killed.

The last coypu was trapped in Feltwell in December 1989, eleven months after they had already been declared extinct. It was ten miles up river from Denver Sluice, where Heath and I had been just a few days before.

I miss them. Granted, as a child I was sold the story of those randy orange-toothed animals vandalising the county and coming for me in the middle of the night, but among rodents, they sure had character. They had appetite, with a partying lifestyle and a horny outlook. What wasn't there to admire?

We continued down the river, paddling the canoe through a marshland of trees known as *alder carr*. It's an impenetrable bog of reeds, briars and densely packed trunks, a half-flooded English mangrove which – after venturing just a couple of dozen yards into it – can be completely disorientating. Twisted stems quickly surround you, while your feet begin to sink, sending up a smell of ancient mud and marsh gas. Stuck there, in the carr, there are brief glimpses of the sky, and occasionally the sound of a motorboat's engine chugs past – a few feet away – but entirely unseen. In the carr, the view is macro. You focus of the lichen growing on the bark, butterflies closing their wings in the sunlight, and the flitting of warblers from branch to branch.

We decided to paddle into it, taking a tiny side channel off the main river into the thicket. The water was as brown as tea and banded like tiger's eye in the sunlight. Fallen trunks had tipped into the channel – each one of them waterlogged and capped with moss, but looking like some form of sleeping alligator. We heard birdsong – probably a band of long-tailed tits – but couldn't see them in the tickertape of leaves above us. The progress was slow – we edged our way and pushed through the overhanging briars. There were many dead ends. As we reversed, our paddles dislodged whirls of inky black silt and bubbles of marsh gas filled the air with a vegetative stink. Heath kept slapping the back of his neck, thinking he'd been bitten, and when we reached a fallen tree he laid his paddle across the boat and waited for me to get us out of there. I suppose he was out of his comfort zone, and I must admit, he's just another one in a long list of people I've put in the front of a canoe and steered – literally – into awkward situations. I paddled with my wife through the swamp in the Mississippi Delta, in the Jean Lafitte Nature Reserve, and she often reminds me (specifically in front of others), that I put her in the bow seat of the canoe in the full knowledge of what was in the water. She was right: ahead of us, through a miasma of humidity and the drapes of Spanish moss, the alligators eyed the approaching canoe through an undisturbed mat of dense green pondweed. No one had been down that particular channel for a very long time and, as we neared them, each one of those little obsidian eyes sank below the surface, with a sinister vanishing act that the alligator has perfected. We became wedged at one point on a raft of vegetation, and one of the beasts surfaced and twisted like a thick oily rope a few feet away. I still remember my wife's shoulders tensing with fear, not just because of what she'd seen, but probably because of the three days I'd already spent winding her up about the dangers of canoeing off piste in the bayou. The alligator dragged itself across the weed, eyeing her like an assassin, then slipped quietly into a hole of black water.

'Now I get it,' she said. 'I'm in the front because I'm on the menu.'

That, of course, did cross my mind when I was choosing which seat to pick in the canoe, but going down that swampy channel in the bayou was also about crossing a frontier into wilderness. On another occasion – in Florida – I was canoeing on a lake called Flint Creek in the middle of a similar swamp, surrounded by another set of ancient trees dripping with Spanish moss. Turtles sat on floating logs. There was strange birdsong everywhere. All around me alligators sunned themselves on the banks, prehistoric and sinister, with their mouths hanging open, and at one point a large male charged into the water and I felt the mass of its body passing beneath the canoe. That slight lift of the boat – as a result of that vigorous reptile travelling at speed a few inches below the hull – was particularly scary, and has left an eerie motion that I can still feel lifting me today, if I want to. The escalation of fears grew worse because, ten minutes later, in the middle of the lake, I found myself entangled in a spindly bush of overhanging branches and there, above me, was a thin and brightly coloured snake. It was semi-draped across interlocking twigs, a bit like a piece of tinsel on a Christmas tree. The canoe drifted imperceptibly until this snake was almost in my eyes, and I had to manoeuvre the paddle somehow, inch by inch through the twigs, to try and extricate myself, without knocking the bush in any way. Several times the handle brushed the wrong stem, and the snake adjusted its balance above my forehead. It watched me impassively, while its tongue – as thin as a single eyelash – flicked through the slot of its mouth.

Later that night, I asked my host about the snake. He said, in calm American understatement, *oh yeah, that's got to be cottonmouth. You don't mess with them.*

I tend to think about that snake every time I'm in a canoe, specifically when my paddle gets tangled in a bush, and I thought about it when Heath and I got stuck between the Broadland trees. That cottonmouth had been a thin ribbon of poison ready to drop onto me, and had summed up the hazards of journeying off the beaten track. Go far enough, and you find the snake. They're waiting for us, patient and cold-eyed, reminding us of primal fears and unwise decision-making. And I wondered whether, in pushing the boundaries of this watery landscape in Norfolk, I would again reach the point where we meet the snake. In the Broads they slide through the reed beds, occasionally opening their mouths in shallow pools to attract any foolhardy fish that will mistake a red throat for a piece of meat. The female adder is said to have another trick of opening her mouth, when threatened, and swallowing her young, in order to protect them. A few years ago, while paddling my family across Barton Broad one summer's evening, I had a suspicion that all was not right in the surrounding water and, a second later, I noticed what looked like a twig propelling itself towards us. It was a grass snake, crossing the broad with its head raised. The grass snake's stare is ice cold and merciless, but in water its eyes can shine like jewels. It passed by the side of the canoe with barely a glance, heading for distant reeds, and I remember feeling simultaneously alarmed and amazed by a creature that shouldn't really be able to swim, crossing a distance that was a bit like a human attempting the Channel. For half an hour afterwards every twig, every floating reed, every whip of grass was a viable snake, too.

Sometimes you go too far, and you end up meeting the snake. But it's also possible for them to slither out of the wilderness, and come into the home. For several years, the house I lived in with my brother was two doors down from Ron's Reptile Shop in Norwich, and snakes were a very present threat in the alley that ran down the back of the terrace. Ron bred crickets to feed his reptiles, and in the warm summer months they escaped the shop and lived behind our fridge, where they happily chirped with newfound freedom. On Saturday mornings Ron would haul the giant boa constrictor out of its pen and dare the local kids to place their hands on the carpet in a row, while the snake slid over them. I put my own hand there once, and the boa moved across it like a rubberised tree trunk, flattening my fingers so that I couldn't push it off me if I tried – and believe me, I tried. Occasionally, a snake would escape from the shop, and Ron would say nothing about it, but we'd see through his window that an aquarium was empty, and we'd know to keep vigilant. We checked our shoes in the mornings. We looked behind the cushions on the sofa. Our neighbour – who was living in the front line of being right next door to Ron's – kept seeing the head of a snake bobbing up and down in a hole in his floorboards where a radiator pipe used to be. He called in Ron, who swiftly managed to coax the snake from the hole, and we were all there, standing in the living room when we witnessed the extraordinary exchange where Ron stood, his legs wide apart, with the bright red and copper chequerboard markings of the captured snake coiled tightly round his hand and wrist:

'Yep,' Ron said, with the brag of a snake charmer that had just helped his neighbour out, 'thass a North American corn snake.'

And our neighbour's reply – one that was almost impossible to say because he was so enraged:

'You can't tell me – *Ron* – you can't tell me *that's* from Norfolk. That's from your shop!'

Ron, who always denied that snakes got out from his aquariums, went on the offensive. 'You lissen here. This ent my snake, right.' He held the snake at our neighbour, brandishing it like a superhero extension of his fist. 'Now you got him mad at you. Don't you start nothin you can't stop.'

A Diff'rent World

After three miles of river, we emerged onto Barton Broad. Heath still looked uneasy in the boat – glad to be out of the trees, but now faced with a wide expanse of water that had different ways of drowning him. Gusts of wind stirred the reeds round the edges, making them look like car wash rollers. The canoe was now being buffeted, while ahead of us we paddled towards dozens of brightly coloured Laser and Mirror dinghies criss-crossing our path, their sails being pulled hard to gain as much speed as possible.

In my early twenties I used to come here with my brother, in our rowing boat: the *Lady Godiva*. We had an outboard fixed on the stern, which we bolted in place so the boat could only go straight. Our method of turning was to sit at the front and, as we chatted, lean one way or the other. It was a surprisingly accurate method of steering, and an image – he and I in our winter overcoats, both bearded, leaning instinctively – that I have often looked back on fondly. Two men enjoying a chat on a deserted wintry broad, while Norfolk passed by at two miles per hour, seems to say a lot about that period of my life, about this part of Norfolk in general, and the way people bend their lives to fit in with the landscape.

'I like it here,' Heath said, out of the blue. He laid his paddle across his lap and stared up at the sky. I did the same, and we drifted quite happily, listening to the breeze blowing in the reeds, then watched a heron glide slowly above the water. Heath wouldn't be so keen if he saw that grass snake coming for him, I thought, realising this was about the same place where I'd seen it happen. On all sides of the broad the banks were dense with thick trees. There were no houses, and no roads or tracks where you might bring a car down to the water. Roads fade out round here, they become narrow, the tarmac breaks up into tractor ruts, then suddenly the whole road vanishes into the marsh. Either that, or they begin to bend in orbital shapes round the Broads – the closer you get, the further it seems you are from reaching your destination. Sometimes it seems like the compass starts spinning in this part of Norfolk.

I remembered a recording made by the BBC in 1947, of the Norfolk folk singer, Harry Cox, performing the *Barton Broad Ditty* in the Windmill Inn, in nearby Sutton. The recording was made at the end of October that year and it already sounds as though the pub's made itself snug for winter, with the noise of logs falling in the grate, pints of ale being put onto wooden tables, and feet tapping on the floorboards caught on the microphone as Harry sings. His voice – sounding as though it's coming from the other side of the room – feels like it's struggling through layers of wood smoke:

> *There was an old man in Barton did dwell,*
> *His name was old Snuffers he's known very well.*
> *He hired the broad till he's fit to go mad,*
> *Don't like the poor fellows should go on to bab.*

The song's about babbing for eels, and how old Snuffers battles with the poachers until he ends up stamping his mark on the eels, pike and bream of Barton Broad so he can recognise what belongs to him. The recording fades in and out as the men listen, but my favourite section is after the song finishes. There's a rowdy cheer, followed by Ernest John Moeran, recording that evening for the BBC, saying: 'Good on you Harry! But Harry, who was old Snuffers?' And Harry Cox replies in a rich humorous voice – full of an accent so thick that it may now have died out from the Broads entirely – that 'Old Snuff that was his nickname, old Henry. Old Snuffers that was his name. He hired the broad. He tried to keep 'em off of babbing. I tell you there's more come in, about. He had these here chaps locked up. He had to go and let 'em out and pay all expense. He had to go and sell his cow to pay it.'

At the southern end of Barton Broad the water funnelled into a single channel, and we began a meandering route as the River Ant wound itself through farmland. We occasionally heard the drone of tractors on the other side of the bank, and passed the entrances to drainage channels that stretched into the waterlogged areas of Reedham and Horning Marshes. I looked for swallowtail butterflies on the thistles and ragged robin – this is the last place in Britain where these magnificent butterflies breed – but only saw the undersides of a thousand poplar leaves that imitated them in the breeze. After dark there is a very different feel to this stretch of river. I've been here many times, paddling a kayak through the night when no one else is around. The water is glossy and black as oil, and the reed beds stand like a long wall of shadow that can't quite be focused on. It's incredibly, undeniably, spooky. And very seductive. In the past, I've turned the kayak into one of the tiny drainage channels and edged my way into the marsh where, on a still night, I've tried to spot one of Norfolk's most perplexing phenomena: a luminous barn owl. There have been sightings, going back more than a hundred years, of owls that noticeably glow with a pale reddish yellow light, sometimes strong enough to illuminate the branches of a tress as they pass. Some of these owls have been shot, and have been said to glow for several hours on the ground, before they fade. Gamekeepers have reported instances of lights hovering in the sky, swooping low over the hedgerows, and flickering as the wings beat. Ferrymen reported that the best time to see luminous owls was on a moonless night in damp weather. Clearly, the skies here are very dark, and odd disturbances in the light are seen often. Will o' the Wisp, Jack O' Lantern, Joan of the Wad, Jenny Burn-tail or Corpse Candle; these are the lights that have flown at people over the years, bringing omens of doom or beckoning travellers onwards into fathomless bogs.

Sitting there at night in the marsh, you can believe anything, not least that owls are able to glow by themselves. One theory is that owls might be picking up a contamination in their feathers, from luminescent fungi in the tree hollows where they roost. I've never seen one. But sometimes, out there in the drainage channel at night, a car's headlights will sweep quickly across the marsh, picking out a twist of rising mist which briefly opens into the shape of wings, and gives you the shock of your life.

We turned onto the River Bure, and paddled along the channel that cuts off the large oxbow of Ward Marsh, now hidden somewhere to the south in dense boggy woodland. Polyurethane cruisers passed us by, nearly all of them with men in a somnambulant state at the wheel, gazing distantly ahead of them while, down in the cabin, their wives wiped down countertops. Sexual stereotyping, rife. Men always at the wheel, women never allowed. It was depressing. We then branched onto Fleet Dyke and into South Walsham Broad, where we'd decided to leave the canoe and take a taxi for the six-mile trip to Norwich. We passed a mooring where I once spent the night in a boat with my wife and kids. I remember how, in the morning, jubilant from a good night's sleep and feeling the world was re-garnished, I wandered along the path to the next boat where a man was sitting on deck having breakfast. He gave me some tea, and we sat in the morning sunshine, listening to the sounds of his wife washing up in the cabin beneath us, and watching the toiling of the ducks and coots across the broad. He told me that he lived near How Hill, and had planned this trip down to South Walsham Broad for months. 'It's a different world down here,' he said, in a reverie of wonder, as if he'd reached the source of the Orinoco. It was the same phrase the man fixing the bolt by the side of the riverbank at Welney had used. Both men overwhelmed by the world they'd strayed into. 'Yep, a different world,' he repeated, this time to himself.

I went back to my family and told them what he'd said, about living at How Hill and bringing his boat down here to travel into a different world. Then I showed them where How Hill is, on the map. It was about two and a half miles away.

Physical distance is not important in Norfolk, I thought. It's the emotional distance that needs to be measured. And the next stage – a trip to Norwich – felt loaded with it.

A Walls ice cream sign, now advertising worms and maggots.

The Bull Pen

I had booked Heath and me into the Holiday Inn on the outskirts of Norwich, where as a child I regularly stayed with my dad and brother when it used to be a Trusthouse Forte. The hotel was eerily similar to how I last saw it, thirty-five years earlier, although a new soundtrack of chillout jazz had replaced the Andy Williams in the reception, low profile lighting had replaced the old spotlights, and a new pattern of geometric carpet had been laid in the overlong corridors. Between the ages of eight and eleven I stayed in this hotel every second or third weekend. We would eat our Friday night meal in the restaurant while, in the car park, a coach would pull up carrying the football team that was going to play against Norwich City the next day. In those days footballers weren't the aspirational lifestyle gods they are now, so the teams from Arsenal or Liverpool or Man Utd got off their coach and wandered quite casually into the hotel and sometimes had a meal alongside us.

We'd eat in the restaurant – always served by the same waitress who'd once said to us: 'Don't mind me, I'm gormless.' So Gormless became her name. She always gave us an extra slice of Black Forest gateau, and my dad would drink the last of the cream straight from the jug to finish it off.

It had been a tiring day on the canoe, so after a quick snack in the restaurant, Heath and I went our separate ways to our rooms. His room was near the reception, whereas mine was towards the end of one of the long corridors that ran through the wing of the building. Walking down it, on a wildly patterned carpet that reminded me of a river full of snakes, I couldn't help picturing how my brother and I used to spend the nights running full pelt up and down this same endless corridor, banging on the bedroom doors, stealing chocolate wafers from the room service trolleys, hitting the lift buttons, and manically buffing our shoes on the automatic shoe polishers. All this, while my dad lay on top of the bed, watching TV, drinking a miniature Grand Marnier from the minibar.

At the end of the corridor I let myself into the bedroom, and wondered whether it was one of the rooms I'd stayed in before. Like all modern rooms belonging to a hotel chain, it was designed to make me feel I'd earned some sort of treat, while also avoiding most semblances of individuality. There were generic photos of abstract art in picture frames above the bed, and writing paper on the desk with the hotel logo on it, harking back to a time when people actually wrote letters from hotel rooms. In the en-suite there was a band of paper over the toilet seat to show it had just been cleaned and, as I looked at the soap dish with its courtesy bath gel and shower cap, I felt part of the tradition of being in a hotel room and wondering what I could steal. These rooms do this to you. They make you feel criminal. I went and stood by the bed, listening to the distant sounds of other people throughout the building. Water passing in pipes, TVs on, doors closing. It was thoroughly odd to know that the last time I'd been in a bedroom here was when I was eight years old, and now I was returning, in my middle age, on a peculiar journey from New York to California which, at that moment, didn't seem to be something I could explain to myself.

I sat in the easy chair by the window and shut my eyes, slightly reeling from the day and knowing that I was in one of those moments when past and present seem to coexist. If I opened my eyes, in this atmosphere-less room, I might see through a wormhole of time into 1977 where, late at night, my dad would be lying on the bed in nothing but his paisley pattern y-fronts, while my brother and I would be staying up late, watching inappropriate films on the TV. It was in a room like this one, and perhaps this very one where, aged seven or eight, I watched *Eraserhead*, terrified, not only by the generally disturbing use of sound and grainy black and white filmstock and the horrific bandaged baby and the awful tortured soul who lived behind the radiator, but also because my dad looked a tiny bit like Jack Nance, who played the title role. My father was oblivious to, he dozed on the bed with his massive chest rising and falling, while his two sons stared in fear at the TV, becoming quietly traumatised.

I spent an odd night at the Holiday Inn, and was glad when the morning came. As I lay in bed, I remembered happier memories about how, on Saturday mornings at this hotel, my brother and I would make an obligatory den using every bit of the room's furniture and bedding, before going to the restaurant to try and outdo each other with the amount of breakfast we could eat. My dad would eat prunes. Lots of them. We'd see the footballers again, walking out to their coach in tracksuits, and sometimes we'd be kicking a ball in the car park when they passed us, giving us a wink and saying *nice one* when we struck the ball well.

I headed to the restaurant, pausing once more to look at the strange geometric pattern on the long hotel corridor on the way. It really *did* look like a river full of snakes. I thought of *Erasehead* again, and how one of

David Lynch's contributions to the cinema is that he has repeatedly filmed the corridor as an eerie hinterland of shadows – a place of transient non-existence, but full of its own unnerving presence nonetheless. This was one of those very Lynchian corridors – full of a thick carpet that might swallow you up, or come to life with its watery serpents, a corridor full of trapped air, closed doors and, no doubt, the fluorescent tube occasionally flickered at the far end.

I reported all this to Heath as we had our continental breakfast, and admitted I was finding it difficult to live entirely in the present. The same chillout jazz tape was again playing from concealed speakers. He nodded, calmly, victim of his own odd night at the hotel, and I asked him if he'd mind if we had a stroll over to the cattle market before going in to Norwich.

'Do you think that will settle your thoughts?' he asked.

'I'm not sure, but it's worth a go.'

We walked across the road, and found the cattle market squeezed into a plot next to the supersized rectangular hulk of a new B&Q warehouse, which seemed like it'd been dropped from outer space. Back in the late '70s the cattle market was larger, a maze of aluminium pens and walkways and gates and roughly tamped concrete, perma-splattered with neon-brown cowpats. It was a baffling place that felt half-empty and half-full at any one time, with wizened-faced men leaning on gates having nothing much to look at, spitting on the ground to emphasise something or other, while from the dark interiors of low sheds you might hear a sudden inexplicable shout followed by a loud crash.

Back then, the market was a bit like a labyrinth and a bit like a climbing frame. The bars of the pens and walkways were as cold as scaffolding poles, and in places the metal was rubbed smooth by the passing of animals. We would run amok through the maze in our trainers, coming across huge slips of urine and poo where we'd have to climb along the gates to avoid them, and every now and then someone would shout *watch out now* and we'd realise that twenty-five sheep were hurtling towards us and – quick as a whip – we'd have to vault out of the way. The sheep would stumble by at speed, nervously looking this way and that, like a rug with twenty-five heads, then vanish somewhere in the maze as quickly as they'd appeared, and we'd have it all to ourselves once more. The sheep were hugely annoying; fast moving and in a blind panic. But the pigs were great. The pigs were always inside the sheds, lying down in the scraps of straw, grunting and twitching when the flies landed on them, whipping their tails. Occasionally one of them would still be chewing a stone it had brought in its mouth all the way from the fields. Compared to the sheep – always nervous near anything with a roof – the pigs lay around in their sheds like they were in an opium den.

As in all auctions, the crowd followed the man with the clipboard, and he would drag them through the warren of market pens like iron filings being pulled by a magnet. The crowd would collect, move on, reassemble, leaving behind a single cow, standing in a pen, unaware that it had just received a death sentence. The 'feathers and fur' auction was a sad experience, birds crammed into cages to be sold as lots, and rabbits hopping about in cardboard boxes, a place where my heart nearly broke when I experienced a man repeatedly trying to wring the neck of a hen, without success.

In the centre of the market were the two cattle rings – brick-built sales rooms where the cows were led round a sawdust pen while rows of Norfolk's butchers eyed them judiciously, and the auctioneer rattled through the rising bids at breakneck speed, on a clanging tannoy, in a heavy Norfolk dialect. In our eyes, it was as if he was in some kind of religious fervour, muttering in tongues while his assistant noticed the smallest of twitches and nods from the butchers dressed in their whites or tweeds.

We sat at the back, terrified to move in case we bought ourselves a cow. It was incredible theatre, and seemed to be a game between buyers giving no movements away and an auctioneer who was trying to induce a fit. In the

middle, the cows would step through a vast weighing scale, and their weights would spring up on a bright red digital readout, before they were led haltingly around the ring, being prodded and pulled each time they stopped. Their eyes were as big as goose eggs and full of emotion, whereas the butchers squinted and seemed to have no eyes at all. The handlers tried to show the animals off, pushing the cows' necks this way and that, and each handler had their own homemade cattle prod – a long stick with a rough nail bound to the end with wire or tape. Some of these prods looked as old as the pikes and spears in Norwich Castle Museum, and the handlers in general seemed a mean bunch, in tight jeans rolled up over huge leather boots smeared with cattle shit.

Occasionally there would be a bull sale, and an imperious Limousin or Charolais would step into the ring, as big as a car, and it would eye the proceedings with barely disguised hostility, taking a step but only when it wanted to, being pulled by the ring in its nose, and every once in a while letting out a giant throaty bellow that reverberated around the building. Some of the old boys would make a half-hearted cheer when the bull bellowed, but everyone knew it was an unequal contest. They were buying the animal, but the animal itself was clearly an unconquerable spirit.

I've thought a lot about those cattle auctions, and the animals that were led through that ritual on their way to abattoirs on the one hand, and breeding herds on the other. How each cow left the ring relieved, oblivious to the mark of death that had just been sprayed on its rump. It makes me feel uneasy, and those buildings are full of this same unease. Too many life and death decisions have been made there for them to be neutral places. Their bricks have soaked up the animal-anguish like sugar cubes. In general I'm far more affected by absence than by presence. I've walked through the first world war battlefields around Ypres in Belgium, stood in the Coliseum in Rome and once, stood in the remains of a cellar in Lidice, in the Czech Republic, where villagers were shot before the Nazis bulldozed the houses and dug up the roads, even removing its name from the maps. In all these places there seemed to be a hotness of absence. A residual trace of what has passed. It had felt indecent that I could walk through, and be allowed to continue.

Standing with Heath in the corner of the B&Q car park, the cattle market was deserted. The aluminium pens were empty, the auction rings looked boarded up, a series of long distance haulage trucks seemed to have been abandoned by the fence, and the only signs we could see were for an upcoming car boot to be held on the site. I thought of the thousands of sheep that had rushed through the market, the pigs in their opium dens and the imperial bulls that had had their moment here, however brief, now vanished. It was full of loaded memories, on a journey that had been teaching me that there is no such thing as a neutral reaction to a place. All that life and hustle and animal fear, it all still existed, but in the realm of the not quite visible.

We were just about to leave, when this man popped up behind me and actually tapped me on the shoulder:

'You bess hurry up – thass goin' on right now,' he said, pointing towards a second building further down the alleyway.

'What is?'

'In that building,' he said, before hurrying off between a gap in the fence.

The second building was at the end of the row, identical to the boarded-up Fat Cattle Sale Ring. I approached it and, at the entrance, heard a strange murmur from inside. A garbled voice, echoed and distorted and, unmistakably, a great exhale of breath. Two concrete staircases curved up from an empty ground floor, and as I began to climb, a cow bellowed loudly. At the top, I entered a full auction room, with fifty or sixty people sitting around a ring filled with deep piles of loose hay. The people were leaning against the steel bars surrounding the ring, or sitting on cement steps radiating up from it. Women and a few children were sitting at the back, on plastic chairs. The building was lit up with fluorescent tubes that gave it a slightly green, sickly glow. It smelt of the hay, cement, tobacco and an odour that might be animal breath.

A needle spun wildly on a large Avery weighing scale suspended from the ceiling, followed by the clanging sounds of a metal pen being rocked beneath it. A gate swung open with a loud crash and a startled bull emerged, led into the ring by a handler prodding it with a hazel stick. The bull was a magnificent longhorn, with thick curls of black hair and a span of horns as wide as a barn door, each one tipped with a darkened point. It stood, resolute, before being urged forward while, from a box at the side, the auctioneer began to rattle through its statistics in a voice where no individual words could be distinguished. This had been the source of the distorted sound I'd heard from the entrance.

The men at the ringside leant forward, intent, assessing haunch and gait with a kind of shrewd appraisal that made me feel cold. It was being sold as a cull cattle, straight to the butchers. Several times the bull seemed to strafe them as the tips of its horns passed between the bars of the ring.

Whether it was the green hue of the light – that gave the room the feel of a faded polaroid – the chant-like calling of the auctioneer's mantra, or the gentle pacing of a huge animal through soft hay while everyone looked on motionless, the auction room felt dreamy and partly mistrustful – as if I wasn't really there. Had I somehow wandered through another junction of time and place where, as I'd entered the building, time had zipped open, and I'd stepped through a portal into the 1970s? There, around me, was an auction room that felt entirely unchanged. Not for the first time on this journey across East Anglia, I felt unable to determine whether I was totally experiencing the present. Looking for clues as to what year it was, all I could see were men in rough jackets and flat caps, an auctioneer chanting into the microphone like he'd done forty years ago, a handler in a long stained coat and jeans, prodding the flank of a giant bull to make him turn. Even the bull itself – looking disdainfully at the crowd, swinging its impressive horns from side to side, seemed complicit. It was a timeless sight, not just belonging to that morning, but to all the mornings over the forty years since I'd last been here. The smells, sounds and textures were all intact, just as I remembered them. And I was briefly afraid to look among the crowd, in case through a jack-in-the-box loop of time I would see myself as a child up there, sitting on the concrete steps at the back of the room, next to my brother and father, all trying to keep still in case we bought ourselves a cow.

Mushy Peas (and How Crabs Have Sex)

Fulfilling my promise, I took Heath into the city centre for his lunch of mushy peas and brown shrimp, served at the open-air market. The market's been in the same spot in Norwich for nine hundred years, is the largest of its type in the country, and the place to go if – for example – you need a boiler suit, fourteen hole AirWairs, watch batteries, old records or curtain fabric. Further in, the market gets down to the business of global street food, delis and pulled pork, as well as the more traditional range of burgers, hot dogs or a floury bap with a limp tongue of bacon hanging from its side. The market is like its own country, with its own particular extra-emphasised dialect – and a breed of people who, while obviously related to those outside, are ruder and free of inhibition.

Heath and I split up, positioning ourselves at different intersections, where we might pick up fragments of conversation.

'Good,' Heath said, 'it'll be like a scene from Francis Ford Coppola's *The Conversation*. I'll be Gene Hackman, and I'm afraid that leaves you as John Cazale. He really had the most incredible shaped forehead.'

I stood next to George's Jacket Spuds, where you can buy 'Breakfast on a Spud' for £4, or a mug of Bovril for 80p. There weren't many people about, and I could only hear snippets of conversation. But my ears began to tune into the local frequency, and at the vape stall I heard: 'I'm abusing my body.' At the chip stall: 'You're looking at over two grand...' Further up, by the vintage clothing: 'Took one tablet so it don't do sod all,' and as I walked past a group of lads by the army surplus I heard (mysteriously): 'No, I'm telling you – you could hide in the toilets.' Further down the aisle I could see Heath outside B's Ts, leaning towards a couple eating a burger. He wasn't being very subtle about his surveillance.

After ten minutes, we re-convened outside the mushy pea stall in Row E.

'Anything?' I asked.

'Actually, yes.' He looked a bit bothered. 'Someone was telling a story – I made a note of what she said: "I came in and there's this pig laid out on the dining room table and I said *what's that there for?* and he says *that's for your birthday, that is.* And it took us two days to eat it."' He closed his notebook, and frowned.

'Extraordinary,' I said.

'Shall we order?'

The mushy pea stall has been here for sixty-five years, and the portions are now being doled out by the third generation of the same family. They serve a hundred bowls a day, rising to a hundred and fifty on a Saturday. I ordered, and when the owner passed me the bowl, I was momentarily disappointed, because it looked like a bowl full of green water. But, like a good quicksand, it quickly stiffened up as I stirred.

'You can ask for a pie with the peas, and she'll put it at the bottom of the bowl,' I told Heath. 'Then she'll ladle the peas over till it's covered. The pleasure being that three minutes later, you re-discover it like a forgotten treasure.'

I've never done the pie-with-peas thing, because I'm not a fan of soggy pastry, and I've never been adventurous enough for a *dripping roll*, also on the menu. For me it's peas only. My only concession is a few teaspoons of mint sauce, stirred in with a ritual figure of eight motion.

While we finished off the peas, I told Heath about another thing I'd once overheard at this market. I'd been trying to get a pair of shoes fixed when a passing girl said to her friends: 'That was definitely rape because I could feel his penis inside me.'

'Really – you heard that?' Heath said.

'Unfortunately, yes.'

After the peas, we walked down through the market, ending up at the wet fish stalls where I introduced Heath to the pint of brown shrimp I'd promised. The brown shrimp is one of Norfolk's finest tastes, and when they are fresh from the sea they are a rival – curled up pretty next to a mound of steaming samphire and tangy hollandaise – for *anything* the world has to offer. Their superb Latin name – *Crangon crangon* – makes them sound like they come from another galaxy... *watch out, here come the Crangon crangons...* They're certainly not the body-built athletes of the shrimp world, but the meat is sugar-sweet and the skin has a dry cracked saltiness that makes them intoxicating. Only Chinese deep fried oysters in chilli and salt can compete for loveliness. Of course the shrimps' size makes them fiddly to eat, but they drive me so crazy that I'm always too impatient to shell them properly. There, I bought myself a pint, and ate them swiftly by pinching them by the legs and biting the meat off their backs, leaning over a bin all the while to drop the remains. At the bottom of the bin I saw a half-eaten crab, and was so filled with crustacean-lust that I briefly considered hopping in like a herring gull and finishing the job.

This wet fish stall often has a sign saying: SORRY, NO SHRIMP TODAY sitting in a very empty tray. Given my obsession, that empty tray is a hard sight to bear, and the fishmonger will always give a full story of why the shrimp boat hasn't been fishing. I've heard excuses about the boat's unreliable engine, a storm blowing up in the Wash, problems with the bolts on the trailer, the sandbanks that have shifted, the truck simply 'hant come' or the shrimp-boiler's 'bruk.' I must have had fifty variants of these excuses over the years, and I'm not sure whether the fishmonger hasn't learnt to recognise me yet, or whether he sees me coming and enjoys the spinning of a new yarn. Whatever happens, he tells his story in one of the strongest dialects in Norfolk, and he tells it with gusto, always leaving me with the image of a single trickster fisherman who seems to be the only man in the county trying to catch the illusive brown shrimp, but who is constantly thwarted by complications of his Toyota's tow bar, the truck's carburettor, the holes in his shrimp nets, his bad knee, his ill-fitting shoes, his misplaced glasses. Together with the mischievous shrimp that appear and vanish on the sandbanks according to the moon, the tide, their whim, and this yarn-telling fishmonger on Norwich market, the fisherman completes the circle of a conspiracy that often leaves me hungry.

I've talked to this fishmonger about other topics over the years, and once asked him how he told the difference between a male and female crab.

'You up for the truth?' he said, with a suggestion that I could back out if I wanted to. I nodded, expecting a simple reply like: 'The fella's got bigger pincers.' What I didn't expect was a full-on sex education lesson.

He grabbed a few of his crabs, turned them over, pulled various parts of their shells apart, before lifting one up right in front of my face:

'See, he got a flap right there. You lift that up and out it... pop.'

The crab obliged with the exhibition, dangling his legs and pincers in the air, bubbling at the mouth like a dirty old man while his nether parts were manhandled. The fishmonger rummaged in his crate once more, this time emerging with one he guessed might be a female. He held the crabs together, rubbing their shells, and I began to wonder what might emerge from various bits of crustacean undercarriage. The male continued to bubble at the mouth. The female looked distinctly unimpressed. As is the way.

'Don't look like he's up for performing,' the fishmonger said, a touch disappointed. The crab swung his pincers in a final unashamed boast. Perhaps the crab enjoyed the whole demo. There's not much to look forward to when you're sitting on a wet fish stall.

Old men bragging about sex is something I associate with this part of Norwich. Behind the church of St Peter Mancroft – next to the market – there is a drop-in centre where anyone is welcome to sit and chat and have a mug of hot chocolate. In the days when I lived in Norwich with little money, this was a place to be on a cold February Tuesday. I once listened to an old man who began to tell me about what Cairo had been like in the war. He told me how he'd marvelled at the range of carpets in the bazaar, the dishes of turmeric and saffron and the dyes used to colour the wools, the smells of tobacco and pots of *ful medames* and *koshari*. And then he talked about the women – how they wandered through the bazaar from one pool of light to another, with a dreamy, dark-eyed expression. He described one such woman, and how he'd leant against woven baskets while he talked with her. Then, with an impish glint that flashed through his rheumy old eyes, he said:

'I took her behind them baskets and slipped her a custard.'

Christ in the Chalk

While Heath took the dog for a walk by the river, I went to the Castle Museum, wanting to see whether its display cabinets still had the power to unnerve me, as they did when I was a child. I was looking specifically for a darkened corridor, leading off the central rotunda, where there were mannequins recreating scenes from East Anglia's Neolithic past. One of the scenes had a small tribe of dirty unkempt people living next to a pond. A male mannequin stood knee deep in the water, holding an impaled fish on the end of a spear made from the jawbone of an animal. He stood there, with his catch, all through my childhood, expressing no particular achievement while, behind him, his wife clutched a filthy child against her hip. There was a suggestion of this woman's breasts, under the rough garment she wore, and an implication of unwashed free sex in ancient Norfolk.

The village looked poor and neglected. At the back of the display the three-dimensional scene reached a point where it continued on a flat painted background. I remember looking at this join very closely. From one position the view made seamless, perfect sense, but when you moved just a few inches to one side, the same East Anglian landscape fell apart, where the 3D hit the blunt misleading wall. When this happened, the scene – and East Anglia itself – felt like a lie.

Next to the Neolithic village, with its idyll of freshly speared fish and available sex, was another display recreating one of the famous flint mines at Grimes Graves. In a claustrophobic tunnel, a life-sized model of a man lay across the rough floor of the mine, holding a deer's antler against a piece of black flint embedded in the chalk. His body was smeared with dirt and there were several darkly bloodied cuts across his ribcage. His face was strained, heavily bearded and anxious, as he stretched for that flint he'd never be able to extract. He looked like Christ to me. Christ in the chalk, who knew a lot about futility and effort and all that was beyond reach.

By his side in the miserable miner's tunnel was a glimmering candle, giving off a thin and pathetic light. It had been made from a fuse wire, flickering to give the representation of a guttering candle. I used to watch that light with a sense of agony, believing that on this side of the glass I should hold my breath in case that candle went out.

I'd imagine every light in the museum would be switched off at the end of each day – the animals and rocks and paintings and porcelain and medieval weaponry would all exist in a perfect undefined blackness, apart from this one flickering wire of light, as the Christ-man tried in vain to touch the flint.

To explain, Grimes Graves is a remote clearing in the centre of Thetford forest, thirty miles south west of Norwich. Surrounded by trees, the site resembles a WWI battlefield, pockmarked with several hundred grassed-over craters, each one marking a Neolithic flint mine. The visitor centre is a draughty place run by a couple of forestry wardens, and I remember going there and noticing that one of the wardens was a small stocky man, with strong forearms and a heavyset face, while behind him was a tall, fair-haired man with a broad smile. Very clearly, these wardens were forest-dwelling stereotypes, the former being the troll, living in a smoky shack in the shadows of pines, while the latter was the merry woodcutter – the trustworthy man who whistled his way through the days. It was so striking that I wondered whether working in a place like this – an island of grass inside a forest – had literally transformed them.

It was the woodcutter who took me to the mineshaft, and I expected to see him on my second visit, a couple of years later. But that time the visitor centre was being run by two women. There'd been a lashing rainstorm that day, and neither of the women seemed keen to sell me a ticket to visit the mine, because it would involve going outside. We waited together for the rain to pass and, eventually, one of them said: 'Shall we go over, then?' She had pale blue eyes and a softly spoken manner. At the mine entrance, she placed a hard hat on my head and seemed on the verge of revealing something. It was oddly intimate. She told me about days spent in the protective shelter built over the mine, watching the rabbits running across the grass in the evening sunlight, and her great empathy for the Neolithic men who had mined their way forty feet through the chalk in tiny galleries, with little more than an antler in their hand and a meal of berries and mushrooms to keep them going. Was she telling me something about her own life? If so, it was cryptic. It began to feel like a confession between strangers, and I had a fleeting awareness that the moment might be more charged than I knew, that she might lean forward and give me a single inexplicable kiss, or was expecting me to place my hand on hers and tell her that everything would be alright.

She waited in the shelter while I climbed down the muddy ladder into the flint mine. The air cooled in layers and a smell of cold damp earth spread around me. The pit was forty-six feet deep and nearly the same in width, and at the bottom was a flat area, with several low-ceilinged tunnels stretching off into the chalk. Spotlights picked out grim fissures and cracks in the walls where flints had been extracted, and I crawled into several of these, recollecting the Christ-like mannequin of the Castle Museum, with his flickering candlelight and his wounded side. All this time I was aware of the woman waiting above me, dreamily looking out through the rain smeared windows.

When I climbed back up she smiled at me, but the moment we had shared before I went down the mine had passed. We walked back to the visitor centre in silence.

I discovered that the Castle Museum had thrown away all its spooky Neolithic displays. Perhaps they'd decided the mannequins were too old fashioned, and that these days kids need buttons and screens instead of being vaguely haunted in the way the Grimes Graves display had affected me. I asked one of the assistants working that day what had happened to the

Christ figure in the chalk. She remembered the display, and kindly referred to the mannequin with the personal pronoun: 'I don't know what they did with him. He was a poor looking sight in the end.'

I wondered. Perhaps the mannequin went on to have a second career, selling trousers in a shop window on Gentleman's Walk, in the city centre, or perhaps his 1970s features and his former life as a Neolithic miner had made him obsolete, even for that. He might have been broken down to his various anatomical parts, and sold as curios in the thrift shops on Magdalen Street. Perhaps he was taken to the landfill site.

During the writing of this book, I wrote a letter of enquiry to the Norfolk museum service. I was told that:

> These dioramas were very dated in content and did not meet the standards expected in modern museum displays.

Suspecting the museum service might have tampered with other displays, I went anxiously into the natural history section, and was relieved to see the giant polar bear was still where he'd always been, stuffed in a pose of ripping apart a seal. This polar bear was shot by Sir Savile Crossley in 1898, while on a hunting trip to King Charles Land, east of Spitzbergen. It looks rabid and ferocious. But I have since learnt that this was not always the case. When it was first displayed in the museum, the naturalist Thomas Southwell found it laughable, writing:

> The most conspicuous addition to the Mammalian collection is a very fine specimen of the Ice Bear... In life this must have been a grand animal, and it is to be regretted that the fancy of the Taxidermist has, by studying to produce a startling effect, given to it an attitude which may occasionally be assumed by a 'begging poodle.'

After this criticism, the polar bear was sent back to the taxidermist to be re-stuffed, presumably with the instruction to *make it look frightening, and less like a poodle*. In my opinion it looks far too scary now, like a Hammer House ghoul, or one of the 'man in a suit' monsters in Scooby Doo.

A similar taxidermic mistake happened with the famous Horniman walrus near my home in London, which was stuffed as plump as a sofa by a Victorian taxidermist who'd never in fact seen a walrus before, and had no other visual aids to tell him what one looked like. All those folds of skin must have perplexed him, so he decided to stretch them out tight, and as a result the Horniman walrus now looks a bit like a giant German sausage.

I was glad that the rest of the stuffed animals were still there, and hadn't been let loose in Norfolk like the Grimes Graves mannequin. The animals filled the gallery in various poses of snarling or pouncing or roaring. There was a great deal of predatory testosterone in there, despite these outbursts of violence being only a fraction of what a life is. It all looked a bit fake, like the tradition of casting generals in heroic poses sitting on horseback.

Among the animals I found something I'd never seen before: a lesser octopus, discovered on my own beach of West Runton, preserved in formaldehyde. It resembled a yellowed section of intestinal tract, with suckers that reminded me of teeth, like the malformed foetal growths that have been known to develop in the bodies of twins. Next to the octopus they'd placed a mummified cat that had been found near Yarmouth. This immediately provoked an unwanted memory for me: when I was six, out riding on a bike alongside my brother in Cambridgeshire, we broke into an abandoned house and, beneath a loose floorboard, we found a mummified cat. The house was close to the animal testing facility at Babraham: the Institute for Animal Physiology. We had heard rumours that sheep had porthole windows surgically implanted into their bellies, so their internal organs could be watched. Finding this mummified cat, so close, made perfect sense to us. Being swaddled like that, and hidden beneath the floor, we knew someone had taken great care with it. In my memory the cat was bound like Tutankhamun, but in all probability the shroud was nothing other than a pillowcase. Memory does that to objects. It warps them over time, sometimes making connections where connections were not necessarily there.

Our pasts are mostly fictional.

Standing there, looking at the mummified cat, I felt I was being stalked. I turned to see three lions in a display case, preparing to pounce at me, with coiled muscles and remarkably tight testicles proudly hanging between their legs. Had the taxidermist used golf balls?

Next to them, in its own case, was an Indian tiger. I remembered this animal from my childhood, and I walked over to the point where it stares you in the eyes, about to leap. As a child, it was just possible to stand here and reach for a button – a domestic doorbell actually – mounted on the side of the case. Press it and the tiger growled. Sadly, the button had vanished, and instead was replaced by some unseen electronic sensor. Nothing seemed to happen. Then a muffled growl began, from somewhere behind the wooden facia of the display cabinet, the same recording of old, mixing with the background noises of teacups being put on saucers, and peewits from the dioramas in the next gallery.

As I left the room, I paused to look at the skeleton of a woman, which throughout my childhood had stood in a curved glass case next to the other animals. She died when she was thirty, the label says, but her bones have already lived on for a hundred more years in this museum, reminding me that we don't know what our bones will get up to after we die. Sometimes they'll outlive us by centuries, like this one, in her glass cabinet listening to the tiger growl fifty times each day. She had recently been moved a few feet round the corner, was now seated and, oddly, an open book had been placed in the skeletal grip of her right hand. Are bones a form of nakedness? I wasn't sure. But it seemed indecent to look at her arranged like this, and I couldn't help thinking that in this latest move she'd suffered a further loss of dignity. She now had the affectation of a high street mannequin, reading and learning when she no longer could, pretending to be something she never was.

I tried to read the passage they'd given her. It was from the *Spectator*, of 1712, a critique of Milton's description of Mammon and Pandemonium, including a passage about being *in a place of torments*. The remains of a dead woman, on display, humiliated, her hand resting on this specific message of torment felt eerie. Perhaps during the night her bony finger had turned to this particular page.

My childhood Holy of Holies was the museum's mineral collection, housed in a dark spotlit corridor, which vastly outdid my own, where the geode of rock crystal – large as a loaf of bread – shone with its own light, the mercury was pooled in a sinister petri dish, and the nuggets of gold were as big as sheep dung. I used to walk past the minerals in a kind of mesmeric dream, learning names, chemical makeups and crystal structures, thinking one day I'd be a travelling geologist, discovering a rich seam of lapis lazuli in a Peruvian hillside, or a waxy opal the size of a goose egg in the Australian desert. As a child I often used to write to the museum, sending them pieces of flint, fossil sponges, sea urchins and unidentified crystals I'd found on North Norfolk beaches. A few weeks would pass, and the specimens would be returned with precise classification labels stuck on them. On one occasion I was allowed to follow my specimen's route through the museum's identification process, and I was led into the empty gallery of estuary and marshland birds, only to be amazed when a secret panelled door was opened between the dioramas and I was invited up a wooden staircase to a brightly lit room filled with rough wooden shelves. There was a long table covered in rock fragments, feathers and pieces of fossils. From that day the museum had an extra dimension to me: the possibility of secret rooms behind the walls. The sense remains that this building – this castle which became a museum – with its galleries leading off its central rotunda, is a building which defies all other buildings: where childhood and adulthood coexist.

The arrangement of sending specimens for identification lasted for several years until, while hunting for amber on the beach one day – I discovered a lump of soft metal. It looked like iron pyrites, but had a crumbling, partly oxidised skin. It was about the size of a small baked potato. It was unusual to find metal ore on West Runton beach, so I brought it home and kept it on a shelf in my rock and mineral collection. I toyed with the idea of sending it off for identification. But then something strange happened: the rock began to grow. First, a white skin developed. Then this skin burst like a rotten fruit, as dark veins of some unknown material began to prise it open from within. For a child who prided himself on knowing his minerals – and once invented a step-by-step guide that could identify the majority of them – this lump of soft living metal had me stumped. More worryingly, I became spooked by it. It was a time of superpower standoff, and this stranger to my local beach had a distinctly nuclear quality. Perhaps not quite nuclear enough to make it glow in the dark, but one that nonetheless felt mistrustful and potentially lethal. I wondered whether it had been spat out from the core of a nuclear submarine, like a sperm whale coughs up a lump of ambergris. After several months of watching it grow in the corner of my room I moved it to the garden shed, to shield me from any gamma rays it might be emitting. For several years more, it continued to grow and change like a rancid cheese among the pots and tools, until it finally fell apart into a soft crumbled pile of ashes in its box. I eventually put it out of my mind. But periodically I thought about it, as one of the unanswered questions of my childhood. Had that mysterious metal ore poisoned me?

It's thought that John Wayne walked over a piece of high-grade nuclear debris in the filming of *The Conqueror* in 1954 – a film so awful that Howard Hawkes spent millions buying up every copy so that no one would ever see it – and contracted cancer along with ninety-one of the film's two hundred and twenty cast who also stood in Snow Canyon that year. There's a photo of John Wayne on location with his sons, showing them the radiation spikes on a Geiger counter he's holding against a rock. The men who cleared the roof of Reactor 4 at Chernobyl wore lead plates strapped across their vital organs, and were told to be out there for no more than fifteen seconds. They were known as bio-robots, because machines had already stopped working due to radiation destroying them. These men did the job, shovelling radioactive graphite off the roof. Some used their hands, picking blocks of graphite hot to the touch, that gave a sensation on their faces of pins and needles pricking them. When they came down from the roof the workers were elated. Within a few months, every one of them had died.

For many years I was likewise convinced I had doomed myself by owning my own piece of nuclear waste. The garden shed felt like Chernobyl itself, requiring its own protective sarcophagus. Only as an adult did I finally send its remnants away, this time to the Natural History Museum in London, with an apologetic letter explaining why I was haunted by this lump of metal. By this time I was expecting it to trigger a full-scale nuclear incident, with the prospect of men in radioactive protection suits lumbering through my mother's foxgloves, and politicians finger-pointing about whose submarine had shat it out.

I realise now it was just childhood hysteria. The Natural History Museum wrote me a very polite letter re-classifying my high-grade nuclear waste as, in fact, unremarkable metal ore, and I ended up throwing the lump away in the pedal bin in the kitchen.

Before leaving the Castle Museum I went to the keep to see the display case which contains a man's skull clearly showing the strike of the axe that killed him. I found it where it always had been, and looked once more at the cranium. It was as smooth as an eggshell, ancient looking, with a sharp cleft across the top, making a blade-shaped gap through which you could see where his brain once was. The stillness of this exhibit, in its little glass case, and the descending arc of violence that once struck it – the life-shattering pain – the cry of rage – made a great impression on me. It felt wrong to look into this man's head, displayed there not because of the life he led, but because of the death that he met. It had a ghostly aura of violence that has never left it.

Nearby, I cautiously approached the most spooky remnant of my childhood: a female Egyptian mummy, standing upright in a display case, with a blackened face as if she had been burnt, with a single hand emerging from the bandages, and a desiccated finger making a half-pointing gesture towards anyone who looked at it. That is a dead body, I would whisper to myself, as a child. Two and a half thousand years ago she was running across the sand in Saqqara, sitting under a shady palm to eat a meal of fresh dates, drinking water from an earthenware bowl with hieroglyphics around the rim. When she died her brain was pulled out through her nostrils and she was entombed in a sarcophagus belonging to a man called Heribrer. The spot directly in front of this display case was easily the spookiest place in Norfolk, and I stood before it once more, wondering what will happen to all these displays, in the end. All these attempts to outwit time, to pretend that we might one day manage it. Heath's German expression came to mind – *Alles hat ein Ende, nur die Wurst hat zwei.* Everything has an end. Only the sausage has two. And perhaps humour's the answer, there's no other way to approach these things. I again thought about the mummified townsfolk of Savoca in Sicily, with their agonised expressions and their tattered clothing, and the knuckles falling from their hands onto the buckles of their dress shoes. Or of the mummified cat pushed under the floorboards in Cambridgeshire, because that cat was loved and the ritual of trying to preserve it was all its owners could think about. Or the photo of the men clearing the radioactive graphite from the shattered roof of Chernoble's Reactor 4. A photo that has outlived all those men, as well as the photographer, and if you look at it closely it's possible to see the radioactivity itself, bleeding up from the base of the frame. A fleeting glimpse of death itself, arriving.

As You aAre Now, Even so Was I

I found Heath in the main aisle of Norwich cathedral, pushing an odd contraption over the tiles: a large, angled mirror mounted on a trolley. In its reflection, he was looking at the medieval carvings on the ceiling, that cover the entire story of the old and new testaments, starting with Adam and Eve in paradise, and ending with various people being eaten in the Book of Revelation's jaws of hell.

'It's pretty depressing viewing,' he said, as I joined him, 'especially if you walk east to west. Go that way and the message is pretty clear – we're on the road to damnation.' He laughed. 'But you do of course have the choice of going the other way – start off in hell and wander towards paradise. Much more optimistic.'

We went into the cloisters and, among the carvings there, we lingered beneath the impish faces of green men and other forest sprites. There are green men all over Norfolk, staring down from pub signs, on ceilings, or as gargoyles on old merchants' houses. All of them tend to have eyes bored out, giving them a piercing stare, and fronds of ivy growing from their cheeks and eyebrows. These ones in Norwich cathedral are particularly expressive, and have been looking down since the Middle Ages, hinting at an ancient religion out there – lurking in Norfolk's woods and heaths – that hasn't entirely been dealt with yet. Perhaps that explains why there are more churches in Norfolk than any other part of Europe. It's a pagan outpost, in need of a lot of infrastructure to keep the witches indoors.

We did a circuit of the cloisters, noting that in some of the carvings there are definitely rude things going on – the medieval mind is never far away from imagining demons prodding naked buttocks with pitchforks – then for a while we sat looking at the elegant spire of the cathedral. When I lived in Norwich, off Cowgate, my bedroom window had a view of the spire, and each night when the floodlights came on, a definite face on it was revealed, with a slotted mouth and two eyes. From my writing desk I used to stare at it and feel it staring back at me with centuries-old judgement. Like all tall medieval structures, Norwich cathedral spire suffers from a slight bend where, over the centuries, the side facing the sun has been hotter and drier than the side facing north. Known as the 'sunflower' effect, the spire has gradually bent a few feet in deference, too. The spire is only fourteen feet lower than the highest point in Norfolk, which is a particularly lovely thought: that all this county's scenery, its woods, fields, broads, heaths and marshes, exist within its range, and the spire can be seen as a graceful measuring stick against the county.

I showed Heath the tomb of Thomas Gooding, who was buried inside the cathedral wall standing up, with the intention of being the first to spring up to heaven when the call came. I imagined him in there, dressed up ready to meet God, with a skeletal grimace, like the freestanding mummies in the monastery in Savoca. Beneath the carved outline of his skeleton is an inscription I've always loved, not just for its grim reminder, but also that it seems to have a gentle inflection of Norfolk dialect written into it:

All you that do this place pass bye
Remember death for you will dye.
As you are now, even so was I
And as I am so shall you be.
Thomas Gooding here do staye
Wayting for God's judgement day.

I told Heath about the church at Little Barningham in North Norfolk where, for hundreds of years, a wooden statue of the grim reaper stood above the front pew as a *memento mori*. Facing back towards the congregation, it looked over the generations with stoic command, giving a skull-eyed look that was – frankly – terrifying. The scythe was held in its hand with a tight grip, while its other hand held an ominous hourglass. The bare bones of its ribcage had a hungry look. The flowing wooden robe hanging from its shoulders had a Darth Vader aspect, but it wasn't in any respect a comic figure. It was death. Death near us. Death will become us. Beneath it was the same inscription as the one on Thomas Gooding's tomb, *as you are now, even so was I*. To carve this figure must have been an ordeal, because at some point whoever had done it – in a nearby medieval workshop – must have realised that his block of oak had turned into something very living, with a troubling presence. The carpenter must have dreaded returning to the workshop each day, where the chisel would carefully carve below those dreadfully watchful eye sockets.

I used to visit this statue on my return to North Norfolk after long periods of being away. On one night I went there with a friend and we walked up the aisle holding a cigarette lighter out in front of us. It was one of the eeriest experiences of my life, with a flickering pool of light beginning to pick out the statue of the Grim Reaper, further up the aisle, and then a malleable aspect to the reaper's expression as we stood before it. My finger burnt, I let go of the lighter, and the quality of that pitch blackness I faced has always stayed with me.

Several years later I heard that, after being there on the pew for a few hundred years, someone came to the church in the middle of the night and cut the statue off with a saw. It was stolen and has never been recovered.

I can only imagine how that reaper must have looked during the moment when it was sawn off the pew. In torchlight, the shadows would have played over the reaper's macabre expression as the thief approached. Then to cut the statue off, the thief must have held the reaper's skull with their other hand. The sound of the saw in the old greasy oak would have been aggressively loud, almost, perhaps, a scream. And at one point, when the saw was nearly through the post, I imagine how it must have been, when the grim reaper moved for the first time in three hundred years. The statue would have trembled, then begun to sway, wielding its scythe above the thief. His new owner.

The Mousehold Commonwealth, or,
The Butcher's Cleaver

We ended our trip to Norwich with a climb up Mousehold Heath, north east of the city, where we sat on a couple of benches overlooking the thousand years of Norwich's skyline. The boxy castle, the two cathedrals – one built for power on top of a hill, and the other an elegant finger pointing to God. Below us we saw redbrick Victorian terraces in grid patterns, surrounding the elegant roofs of 18th century merchant houses, and along the river the rigid outlines of modern industrial units. Norwich has an overwhelmingly benign quality: a patchwork of flint and brick, medieval and quiet, with polite traffic jams and well-maintained trees. Norwich is a soft looking city. It will look after you; give you a good life. Even the street names suggest secret qualities of warmth and humour: *Golden Dog Lane, Rampant Horse Street* and the vaguely rude *St Gregory's Back Alley* – names from a city that has been gently amusing its occupants for a thousand years.

Built across the top of the hill is the imposing façade of HM Prison Norwich, which now hosts the Britannia Café, where your tea and scones are brought to the table by Category D inmates. Heath thought we should have a cream tea there and plan the last stage of the journey. I kept it quiet from him that in my early twenties I did six months as a teacher in this same prison, running – among other things – a film club, and that during a screening of *Philadelphia* (as part of national AIDS week), one of the inmates had shouted: *oi gov what's this faggot shit!* before he let off a fire extinguisher in the room while his mate stood on the table, pulled his jeans and pants down, and bared his bumhole at me.

This was the prison where I once shook the hand of Britain's oldest murderer, who – although his lungs were wheezing with emphysema – sat in his cell taking pride in giving visitors an extra-strong, lingering handshake, letting you know that it was the squeeze of a strangler.

It had been a place of contrasts. Among the Larkman estate thieves and Thetford joyriders, there'd been asylum seekers awaiting deportation, one, an incredibly softly spoken man from Mozambique whom it would be difficult for anyone to find fault with. He was there, sitting calmly at a table learning to read the captions under magazine pictures, while the swaggering lads of Norfolk had farting competitions around him. And I remember a fellow teacher of mine – a wonderfully kind and enthusiastic man called Eric – and the morning when he walked into the teaching session to find fifteen highly muscled black guys – newly arrived from Belmarsh prison – leaning back in their chairs on the far side of the room.

'Hi, everyone,' he said and, to break the ice he launched into: 'My name's Eric, which is an Anglo Saxon name that means *kingly*.'

After a very long silence, one of the new inmates – covered in tattoos and dreads – leant forward and grinned:

'My name's Le-roy, which means *the* king.'

Mousehold Heath was the spot where Kett's army of sixteen thousand peasants amassed, ready to sack Norwich in 1549. Their rebellion became known as the Mousehold Commonwealth, and looking across the heath it was easy to imagine the fires of their camps and a night where they might have wondered what would happen the next day when they marched on the city. Would they be the beginnings of a revolution that would sweep across Britain? Many of those peasants had never been to Norwich before, and it must have laid itself out before them like a fabled city – full of church spires and grand houses and being totally unfathomable to a worker who had only known hedgerows and village life.

One of the events of Kett's rebellion has always amused me. It happened during a skirmish in the city, when Lord Sheffield – leader of the government forces, fell off his horse and reached out for his white handkerchief to arrange his own surrender. Before he had a chance, a butcher from Cromer called Fulke hacked him down with a cleaver, probably because no one had ever told him what a white flag of truce meant. Fulke must have seen the aristocrat and simply thought *this is it lads, here come one of them*, using one of his meat cleavers, because that's what a butcher would use. I suppose someone else nearby must have said: 'Heh, Fulke, you shouldn't really have done that – the bloke was surrendering,' because Fulke promptly left the battle, embarrassed, and proceeded to walk back to Cromer, his part in European history done with. Behind him, in the ruined streets of Norwich, he'd left the slaughtered body of a nobleman, and an insurrection that now had no hope of peaceful resolution. The conflict suddenly escalated with the arrival of a much stronger government force, and Kett ended up hanging in a gibbet from the castle walls.

If Fulke hadn't swung that cleaver, then maybe Kett could have negotiated terms with his prize prisoner, or prepared his forces more effectively, and European socialism might have been born right here on Mousehold Heath, instead of having to wait a few more hundred years for Marx and Engels to write their manifesto. Oh, the old Cromer butcher! You should've stuck to selling sausages.

Thurne River

Early next morning – after a second night at the Holiday Inn – we returned to our canoe and set off for the Thurne River, which would take us to a point five miles north of California. With Heath in the front, Half-Shandy in the middle, and me in the back, we paddled quietly out of South Walsham Broad towards St Benet's Abbey. I was glad we'd been to Norwich but relieved, also, to be back on the boat. A city is something to get lost in, whereas a river is something to follow, and California at last seemed to be within reach.

The water was calm, and we paddled through a thin, early morning mist, watching herons standing silently beneath the trees. Our paddles dipped with regular rhythm. The river began to pass so slowly that, at times, it seemed as though the journey might advance at microscopic pace. I noticed a single reed for a whole minute, and still it hadn't passed. Norfolk at this rate appeared laid out in its individual atoms. Another few reeds passed by. Half-Shandy looked over the side at a duck nibbling grass on the bank, then put his head down again.

What had I been expecting to find in this journey? I began to wonder. The start and end points – New York and California – felt like they'd been chosen with arbitrary haste: two pins we could push into the map, and string a thread between them. Did a connection need to be found? Or was it the journey itself that was the purpose? It was exactly a week since we'd started the journey, and already the fens, in particular, felt distant and unknowable once more. The fens had felt stark and mysterious – and crossing them had given me a feeling of having encountered the ghost-lives of my family, all of whom had left that particular landscape now. The North Norfolk coast, in contrast, had felt rich with my own memories, and had been filled with a luminous quality of light and a beguiling sense of soft erosion. The trip south through the Broads had felt meditative, as though I was entering the heart of an East Anglian landscape that beat its own rhythm. Then Norwich, a trickier presence, layered with conflicting experiences and not something I could readily decode. Perhaps only at the end would I see the journey for what it truly was.

As we turned into the River Thurne we could hardly tell the direction of the flow. These Norfolk rivers are virtually stationary, and due to the lattice of drainage channels and water pumps surrounding them, half of them don't know which way to flow. Sometimes the water makes the sensible choice of flowing towards the sea, but at other times it reverses, flooding inland with a high tide. And the Thurne is a peculiar river because its source is virtually at the coast, from where it makes the baffling decision to flow inland for its entire length, before joining the Bure and twisting back towards the sea in a wide semicircle.

Unlike the River Ant, the Thurne is tidal, and one of its characteristics is that twice a day the incoming seawater messes up the fish – the saltwater floods in and the fish make a dash upriver to escape it, often hiding out in the boatyards. Sometimes they'll get caught and, gasping for oxygen, a whole stretch of the river's fish will float to the surface and expire. It's an eerie sight, and can make you feel that, below the surface, something else is going on, beyond your understanding.

For seven miles it flows through a very flat and rural part of Norfolk, and there are moments when the entire river seems to lift higher than the fields. Standing on the bank, you can look at a view across a flat ploughed field, several feet below you, which suddenly becomes even stranger when a sail begins to slide through the soil in the distance. A boat, travelling on a hidden channel. It's just another example of Norfolk's deceptive landscapes: if you set off across the saltmarshes you find yourself thwarted by a labyrinth of creeks; set off across the Broadland marshes and you similarly find yourself in a maddening lattice of drainage channels. The view looks endless – it looks like you could walk for miles and miles until you reach the sea, whereas in fact you'll be lucky if you can walk a couple of hundred yards before you meet a drainage channel that blocks your path.

The people who live here have an acute understanding of these beguiling distances. A house may be a ten-mile drive away from its neighbour, even though they are forty feet across from each other on either side of the river.

At Repps we entered what Arthur Ransome called 'a water street,' where on both sides of the river there was a string of chalets and boathouses running for about a mile. Behind the houses was a single cement footpath, but no road, and most of the homes still use the river for transport. Each house had its own dock, a stretch of river frontage, and lawns splattered with duck and goose poo. The Broads is now a national park, with strict planning laws, but many of these chalets were built when any farmer thought he could knock together a few planks of wood, nail corrugated tin on the roof, and rent it off as a retirement dream. Over the years this water street has become more established, but it still has a shanty feel.

It must be a strange place to live. With nothing but empty fields behind them, the water streets of Repps and Potter Heigham are densely populated, with the chalets crammed together with just enough room between the plots to angle a paintbrush when repainting the clapboard with creosote, but not much more. In the height of summer these houses are passed every minute or so by a broads cruiser, and when Heath and I paddled through the street, we felt constantly watched from the array of deck chairs and sun loungers facing the river. It felt oddly confrontational. It's all very strange: to move here seeking remoteness, then live cheek by jowl with so many others who've come here for the same reason.

Some of the chalets had a Spartan look – neatly varnished, surrounded by manicured front lawns, barbecues trussed up in rain-covers, and miniature fences to repel the ducks. But others appeared to be groaning under the weight of accumulated knick-knacks and ornaments – windchimes hanging from the eaves, plastic frogs on the lawn, cement wellie plant holders, flower pots in the shape of swans or wooden wheelbarrows, hedgehog foot scrapers and ornamental birds standing on the patio or nestled in the flowerbeds. Some of the chalets were so cluttered it seemed they might be emanating some sort of magnetic attraction for the world's unwanted possessions.

.

Living by the water must bring these characteristics out. It attracts the eccentric and the recluse in equal measure, which is a common story throughout the Broads. Nestled into the reed beds it's still possible to find ramshackle cottages, where the kitchen floor is uneven with age, the shelves are propped up with books, an open fire burns for half the year and the windowsills are lined with homemade jams and preserves. Outside, there's a broken down swing among the brambles, and grubby-faced children race about half-feral, having a crazy idyllic childhood riding bikes through an orchard. The ivy grows up the walls and into the house, and the chairs and sofas get pulled out of the living room and spend the summer outside. Nature drifts in and out of these houses along a permeable border.

And yet, a little way along the riverbank, there'll be a totally different type of home, referred to by one of my friends as: 'Norfolk Tidy.' These houses are immaculate. Neater than neat. Their gardens are micro-clipped – almost as if nail scissors have been used for the job, with perfect hair-dressed shrubbery, and roses that are deadheaded before a single curling petal has a chance to fall. The house itself has double- or triple-glazed polycarbonate windows, and such excellent draught control that when you open the front door you clasp your hands to your ears, because they've just popped with the pressure. *But I'm not equalised*, you think, as you venture in. You can spend the afternoon in a living room that is hoovered daily, on a stiff sofa that faces a nest of tables, and listen to the ticking of a clock while, through the window, you glimpse an outside world that looks suspiciously as though a photo's been projected there.

These houses are a kind of insulated spaceship, with airlocked porches and magnetised cat flaps to make sure that the outside stays where it belongs. Outside.

The border between a countryside that smells of cow parsley, chamomile and ripening barley meeting a firmly closed bathroom window where – inside – there's an air freshener smelling of artificial honeysuckle, is an interesting one, and it's easy to be dismissive about these houses. But perhaps there's something more nuanced going on, about people who may have grown up in draughty homes finally having a chance to create a bubble of air they can control. Heating bills are kept at a minimum, dust is marshalled and dealt with, and you can sit at a window and know that bacteria and smells and mud are things that won't come in. You think you have controlled and tamed the raging chaos of nature. But wait... outside, the forsythia dares to put out a trembling leaf! You see the leaf emerge, you don the gardening protection gear, go through the airlock, and prepare to micro-clip.

Heart of Darkness

The tiny arch of Potter Heigham's medieval bridge loomed ahead, its stonework gouged by several hundred years' worth of boats squeezing through. At low tide it's possible – after de-rigging a mast, collapsing a cabin and remembering to lie flat on the deck yourself – to get a boat as large as a Norfolk wherry through this hole. I did this once, and remember how strange it was to see the old stones of the bridge passing a couple of inches above my eyes, after so many miles of open sky and watery landscape. The river pilots like to drive the arch at speed, showing their skills, even though at high tide nothing more than a kayak can get under. Some boats manage to get themselves wedged. My own collision with Potter Heigham Bridge happened when I took my family for a week on the Broads, hiring an old wooden cruiser. I had my eye fixed on the stone arch from a long way off, and was so transfixed by the small slot of river water beneath it, that I was entirely unaware of the second bridge at Potter Heigham – the modern road bridge. I saw the brutally low span of its steel girders too late and, even though I put the engine into full reverse, the boat glided – in the unstoppable motion of a nightmare – until the girder passed above the deck and smashed into the cabin, removing it from the boat like slicing the top off a boiled egg.

I didn't tell this to Heath – he was already questioning my boating skills at regular intervals – but this stretch of river still has that nightmarish quality to it, of a motion that can't be stopped and an accident that's so imminent the crunch of old wood and glass plays in a loop every moment I return here. The stretch of river feels haunted, which is appropriate, because Potter Heigham Bridge is also the scene of one of the Broads' more graphic ghost stories. It was here where Lady Carew and her daughter, Evelyn, decided to sell their souls for the purchase of a love potion, to ensnare the eligible bachelor Sir Godfrey Haslitt. Their plan worked, and Evelyn married her beau. But there was a catch (because there is always a catch when you sell your soul), where on the night of her wedding, a phantom coach driven by skeletons took the bride away, and as it raced demonically over Potter Heigham Bridge it burst into flames.

Upriver from the bridge, the Thurne enters a vast shallow dish of Norfolk, crosshatched with hundreds of drainage channels, dykes and reed beds. Somewhere in this labyrinth was the river's source, and as we entered this part of its system I had the feeling that water was beginning to flow at us from every angle. Along the northern bank, the last of the river streets came to an end, and the Thurne became entirely ours. At Martham, I saw the boat yard where I hired the broads cruiser – the one I crashed into the bridge – and the stretch of quay where I had to return it to them with its cabin hanging off the side. The boatyard had a few wooden cruisers up on bricks, covered with tarps, and was clearly a place where nothing much happens from day to day and year to year.

This area is well known for its isolation, and I whispered to Heath that if we were lucky we might spot someone who's never left the village in their life. I was thinking of one such man who was working at Martham boat yard when I last went there – and as Heath and I passed the yard, I did indeed see him again, in his long, worn blue overalls, carefully applying varnish to a section of a boat's hull. I hadn't seen him for ten years, and the last time I saw him he was doing exactly the same job. He'd looked old before, so didn't seemed to have aged now, but to see him with the paintbrush again felt like an affirmation of all he stood for, and I idly wondered whether he was in fact re-applying the varnish to the very same piece of wood that I'd seen him treating last time.

I remembered the exchange I'd had with him back then. He'd asked where I was from, in strong dialect with the traces of a stammer.

'North Norfolk,' I'd replied. 'Near Cromer.'

He'd rubbed his temple with a varnished finger, nervously, and looked out across the marsh, before saying: 'Oh – thass hilly up there, int it? Real hilly,' as though I'd grown up among some kind of East Anglian Alps.

Heath and I turned left, towards Hickling Broad on Candle Dyke. The river widened into a network of reed beds, water channels and ditches. Clumps of river weed – known locally as *hover* – began to pass by, floating dense on the surface, as thick as mattresses. Each one seemed like a prototype island, that might coagulate into new land. Then Hickling Broad opened up in front of us, like an inland sea, fringed with reed beds. It seemed the only elements here were sky and water, with land as thin as an eyelash between them.

I began to think that going upriver like this, leaving behind the strange communities of the Norfolk water streets and entering a wilderness of floating swamp, we might be journeying into our own East Anglian heart of darkness. Maybe there was a well spring of madness ahead, where people had grown native and feral, at the source of the flow. Hickling's own Mr Kurtz, hiding among the reeds; and me becoming Charles Marlowe, drawn to the 'blank spaces' on the maps. Hickling Broad certainly encourages you to think this way. I spent the night on this broad once, in an old wooden boat anchored to a mud weight. After watching the sunset fade, I saw herons and egrets fly by lazily, losing themselves against a limitless sky. As dusk fell nothing more stirred. It had felt like Africa, in the middle of England.

It's the largest of the broads and has little around it – no hills, no woods – and, like any large body of inland water, Hickling Broad tends to control the microclimate of its surrounding area. On a cold February day, it is a bleak and challenging place. But on a hot June afternoon, the water becomes a single sheet of mirrored sky, and the distant reed beds give the land a feathered-at-the-edges texture. The broad fills the area with a feeling of soporific bliss. People walk up to the water, they slow down, their heartbeats calm. The sun sets over the old thatched boathouses nestled in the reeds, and for a full hour everything turns golden and waxy, as if you've stepped into the glossy composition of a calendar photo. You cannot move. You look at the view, spellbound. You become the fly in the bead of amber. It claims you, and you don't resist.

Reaching the northern tip of the broad, we tied the canoe to the quay outside the Pleasure Boat Inn. Heath climbed out, wearily, claiming his back was broken, and said Half-Shandy needed to chase something. He walked off down a path alongside the boathouses, clutching his lower back, and I saw him peer into one of the boat builders' yards. I heard the sound of a distant power tool. Three swans glided towards the canoe, looking aloof and cold-hearted.

It was already two o'clock in the afternoon, we still had a fair distance to go before we reached California, and I was beginning to wonder whether we'd get there in daylight. California-in-the-dark seemed like it would be the wrong way to finish the journey. I went into the pub with the plan of picking up some sandwiches for myself and Heath, and thought that while I was there I'd take a look at the stuffed pike that's always hung near the bar.

The pike was above the door to the saloon, where I remembered it. It was huge, with tobacco-coloured skin and a long curving mouth. I had the feeling that after a few pints at the bar, this pike would begin to look like it was grinning.

The stuffed pike from the Pleasure Boat Inn. A 14lb fish caught by R.E. Barnard on Heigham Sounds on 24th December 1954. Now fixed above the door of the dining area, next to a straw sombrero.

Near the stuffed pike was a display of photos dedicated to the local gun club. A frame had been built around them made from shotgun cartridges. On one of the pictures a woman had been given a handwritten speech bubble, which said: "Good to have a proper weapon in my hand for once!!" But what struck me about the pin board was how – across the collage of photos – the members of the gun club seemed to be levelling guns at each other, some aiming straight for the back of another one's head.

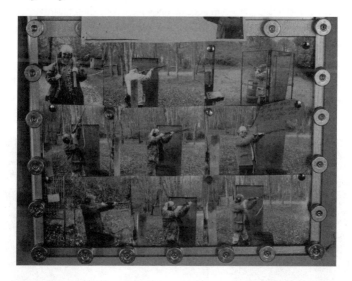

A lone man sat at the bar in a thick twill shirt, nursing a pint. I ordered my sandwiches and started talking to him about the pike hanging above the door. 'Used to be two pike in this pub,' he said, 'but one got stole after a party.' He told me that on the last day of the fishing season he'd been: 'out on a jolly on Ormesby Broad – and we got us eight pike in four hours.' He went on: 'There ent many of the great fish left. And them that's left are canny – but if you land on their noses they'll come out of the water and grab it.' He shot his hand out to snatch the air above his pint, to demonstrate.

He nodded to himself, then glanced at the stuffed pike: 'In the roof of their mouth there's this plate and there's literally hundreds of teeth in there and if they do catch you they've got this anti-coagulant and you will not stop it from bleeding I tell you that.'

'You've been bitten by a pike?'

'Oh yeah, I've been bit by them.' He pointed to various places on his hands. 'But you turn them on their back there's this V where the gill plates are, and if you get a hold of that they han't got no choice but hold their mouth open. If you think about what they are – a predator and all that – they're not as hardy as you might imagine. It don't take long to kill them. That's why we won't use barbed hooks – we buy hooks, we break the barb off.'

'Here, look at this,' he said. He showed me a photo on his phone of his own stuffed pike, hanging above the door of his living room. 'Bought that on eBay from a snooker hall.'

His fingers smelt of cigarette smoke, and as he began to swipe through more photos, I saw pictures of his living room, where an entire wall was covered with stuffed animals and birds in homemade display cases. Next to the stuffed animals was a giant flat-screen TV, where I could see some sort of gameshow playing in a blaze of colour and light that flared across the photo. I imagined him sitting on his couch one evening, watching the telly, and reaching for his phone to take these odd pictures of his room. It seemed his life wasn't shared with anyone, and the moment of him choosing to record it like this felt revealing. It said a lot about loneliness and a lot about being a man out here, in the Broads. Just him and his stuffed animals and, when I looked closer, the head of a golden retriever sticking in from the side.

'That one's not stuffed?' I asked.

'Oh him, no. Not yet.'

He said it with the barest hint of a joke. He continued to scroll through his photos, proudly showing me one of a barn owl he'd bought in a car boot, which he'd mounted in a glass-fronted Technics hi-fi cabinet. As he put his phone away I noticed his homescreen was a photo of himself, brandishing a shotgun in the reed beds.

I wondered whether I'd found my very own Mr Kurtz, after all, at this furthest point upriver; the true heart of Norfolk's darkness. And his living room, with its trophy wall of stuffed animals in homemade display cases, alongside a huge plasma TV, was like seeing the heads on the spikes at the upper reaches of the Congo. Sitting there, on his black leather sofa, holding his camera phone up to the dead animals and the TV, I imagined him saying: this is it, this is my home, the horror....

Anglian Alligators

Back in the canoe I told Heath how I'd found Mr Kurtz, sitting on a bar stool at the end of the river, and that Mr Kurtz owned a bungalow with a massive TV surrounded by heads on spikes and stuffed animals in homemade display cases.

'Well done, *Marlowe*,' he replied. 'You must add those details to your report.'

'Next trip we do, Heath, we should visit all the stuffed pike in Norfolk. There's one at the Barton Angler pub, one hanging above the "drinking corner" at the Kings Head in Coltishall, this one here at the Pleasure Boat Inn, one at the Bridge Hotel in Potter Heigham, I think there are some at Lathams fishing shop, one at the Geldeston Wherry and a whopper at the Castle Museum.'

We paddled on in silence into the centre of the broad, and again I noticed Heath getting uneasy about the amount of open water around him.

'Pike can jump clear of the water, Heath, did you know that?' I said.

'No, I didn't know that.'

'They might go for your hand. It's quite low on the paddle.'

'You can stop that kind of talk.'

'Just saying.'

He splashed me. But I saw him move his hand higher.

Pike have been known to bite the feet of herons, perhaps mistaking the grey-green toes for roach or dace in the shallows, attack rats on the bank and drag them into the river, leap clear of the water to pluck frogs from the reeds, and will stalk a line of ducklings all day like a U-boat picking off ships in a convoy.

They are one of the only fish in England that can fully breach the water when they launch their attack, and for an astonishing half a second can be seen levitating like a zeppelin in the sunlight. Even their Latin name, *Esox Lucius*, make them sound like a comic-book villain from Gotham City.

To look at it, the pike is an incredible design. It's as slim as a torpedo, with forward-facing eyes and a strong, no-nonsense tail that can give it – with one powerful flick – incredible acceleration. Apart from the dorsal, stuck right back near the tail, the rest of its fins are tiny, to reduce drag, and the pike can probably not turn very efficiently. Its head is covered with armoured scales that look like they could stave in a rowing boat. In close combat it must be formidable. Lurking under floating mats of reed, or in the shadows of river pools, it must come at you as though it's shot from a speargun, with gill slits edged with spikes and an open jaw lined with needle sharp teeth. And more teeth in the roof of its mouth. In the hand, it can play dead, then suddenly lurch and take the tip of your finger off.

The largest pike caught on Hickling Broad was a 30lb fish caught in 1956, which recently sold in its display cabinet for £4,500. It was four-feet long, and the angler, Donald Tate, described the moment he caught it:

'The pike really frightened me. It came straight out of the water and crashed back with the noise of a ton of coal being emptied.'

Yet despite its fearsome reputation, I remembered what I'd been told about them being surprisingly delicate, and that despite all that impressive armour and weaponry, the pike will quickly die if handled. These Anglian alligators are more vulnerable than they make out, and perhaps it's something they realise. It's only after they're stuffed and mounted in the display cases, with teeth revealed in a cunning smile, that they become the fish we want them to be.

Thinking of those photos taken by the gun club, displayed in the Pleasure Boat Inn, I decided to include this picture captured by my grandfather, of his dog sitting beneath a dead hare. The dog looks watchful, but his shadow looks strangely downcast, and the hare's shadow looks alert and ready to spring from the hook, like a sword of Damocles. It suggests many things; the dog's patient loyalty and willingness to guard the corpse, and perhaps my grandfather's admiration for the tableau of dog and hare. But what's startling about this photo is that he took it in December 1918, just a couple of weeks after returning from Belgium after the war. Photos before and after it on the film show men in puttees and great coats waiting at train stations. And I think of my grandfather, in the quiet moment when he took this photo of his dog and the hare he'd shot, and then of him a few minutes earlier, hunting among English hedgerows, scanning the bare fields along the sights of his shotgun, so fresh from war, and wonder what he really saw when he pulled the trigger.

Billy down the Rabbit Hole

As we paddled into Horsey Mere, I realised our journey was nearly over. To my left the Waxham New Cut entered the broad, its water red with clay, as dark as old blood in a long dead vein. Ahead I could see the Horsea Drainage Mill where we planned to tie up the boat, before the final five mile walk south to California. I thought of my journey so far, and in particular the characters I'd come across. There was the man in Boston marketplace who sold his head to science before he died, spending his Saturdays running round the market stalls, frightening children and making young couples look the other way. He'd felt like an impish presence at the start of the journey, a twilight character giving me a wink, but so much on the fringes that to try and look at him made him vanish. Then as we travelled under the giant sky of the fens, that other exhibitionist had appeared, Daniel Lambert, the heaviest man in history in 1809, touring Lincolnshire in his specially strengthened carriage, charging a shilling a view. His route through the fens had coincided with ours at various points, and I wondered how he must have felt out there, sleeping in coaching houses, with his vast chest rising and falling in the middle of the night, waiting for the visitors who would pay to see his body the following day. Lambert's story felt lonely to me, but in all the research I've read, he apparently lived his life to the full, so maybe the suggestion of a lonely man out there in the fens was only an invention of mine, and shouldn't be trusted. But I did feel the melancholy air that surrounded that other tragic character – the vicar of Stiffkey. I felt the vicar's doomed presence as I walked through his parish on the North Norfolk coast, and rushed past his tombstone, afraid of the sour air from a man who'd gone to his grave in such a way. There was

Samuel Birley Rowbottom, peering through his telescope at a flat Earth, Noel Edmonds winking at me from a slot machine at the Brewers Fayre, and at the Adrian Flux arena, a procession of souped-up hearses that reminded me of the mummies at Savoca, Sicily. Then a walrus that may or may not have swum up a fenland river, and whales that had appeared and vanished on Norfolk beaches. A sun fish, too, glimpsed in a window's reflection, being carried to a taxidermist's. In Wells I'd glimpsed the Dutch skipper of the *Albatros*, and known that in a parallel universe he might have been the last person who'd seen me alive, after I fell from his deck crossing the North Sea. In Walsingham I'd been aware of something eerie and inexplicable in the eyes of the doll-like statue in the Holy House. In Sheringham – after the long quiet miles of walking along saltmarshes and shorelines – I'd imagined the swaggering banter of all those vanished fishermen: Belcher Johnson, Loose-Gas Knowles, Scratchums Pegg and Bumshee West. All long dead and gone, but their voices had sprung at me like a radio dial that had slipped onto a crazy talk show, as they yelled each other's names across the slipway, swinging ropes and horsing around. Between the crab boats I'd imagined their old faces – squinting at me with eyes set like small cuts of flint, half-hidden in clouds of smoke from clay pipes.

In Norwich I'd imagined the heavily plodding gait of that Cromer butcher, Fulke, heading back to the coast in 1549. Old Fulke, still carrying his bloodied cleaver, feeling a bit ridiculous and a bit proud of the murder he'd done, knowing he'd played some part in history, but not really fully understanding it either, and really just wanting to go back to his shop and sell sausages. Everything has an end, only the sausage has two; Fulke would've liked the saying.

Some of these figures have been glimpses into another time, like the lost mannequin of the Grimes Graves miner in the Castle Museum, or the grimacing-snarling-smiling face of the woman from Saqqara who became mummified and now looks out forever from her display case, the green men that peer down from the roof of Norwich cathedral, or the vanished grim reaper of Barningham church. By Norwich marketplace, I'd remembered that rummy-eyed old devil who told me he'd *slipped a custard* to the woman in Cairo, during the war. And in Hickling I'd felt a fleeting recognition of my very own Mr Kurtz – the hint of madness that stalks men who live an isolated life.

I realised I had, in fact, taken several journeys from New York to California. The easiest journey to understand was the one that followed a route across a map: I was at this place at this time and then I went there. But other journeys had happened, like the one through parts of a childhood I can't quite remember in specific detail, or the ones through my parents' and grandparents' lives, from the photos I'd found and the fragments of lives I'd heard about. And yet other journeys, too, glimpses of oddities and stories and parts of stories that may or not make sense when written up in this book. I was a curator as well as a traveller, and my particular route had been only one of many possible paths. If I started a journey from New York to California again, the result would be different each time. Like particles in a Brownian motion experiment, interaction with the environment is random, and a path will always be different, it cannot be predicted and it cannot be reproduced.

We tied the canoe up at Horsey Drainage Mill, and began to walk south along an empty lane towards the village of West Somerton. It was good to be off the boat, but the late afternoon sun was beating down on us and the fields had an oppressive dust of pollen hanging over them. There was no one around, and it began to feel like we'd arrive in California and find it deserted.

At West Somerton we went straight to the small flint church of St Mary's, to see the famous tomb of Robert Hales, the Norfolk Giant, who'd been born here in 1813. He was one of nine children, all of whom were over six-foot tall. One of his sisters reached the height of seven-foot, but Robert kept on growing, outstripping his siblings until he reached the giant's height of seven-foot-eight. Not only that, but he weighed an impressive thirty-two stone. After being paraded in Norwich's Tombland fair, then at the freak shows in

Great Yarmouth, and being introduced to Queen Victoria and Prince Albert as the tallest man in England, he was taken to America to tour with Barnum's circus. There are rumours that he was coerced into marrying a seven-foot man, who was dressed as a woman for the wedding, and a further hint of bigamy, during his eventual return to the village where he was born and where, exhausted, he died at the age of fifty.

His tomb couldn't be missed. It was a stone sarcophagus on four legs, shaped like a bath tub, standing at the edge of the churchyard, bearing the inscription that begins with:

Beneath are deposited the mortal remains of
Robert Hales the Norfolk Giant.

It was strangely quiet in the churchyard, and I couldn't help feeling bothered by a fairy-tale notion that the giant was asleep, inside his tomb. By my estimation, the stone box was less than seven feet long, meaning he must be in there with his knees bent up. Either that or a semi-sitting position, which gave me a troubling image of him pressing his ear against the lid. I took a step back, and then realised that all around us, in the grass, were the graves of his supersized family – his tall parents and giant siblings and, further across the churchyard, with unnerving coincidence, the graves of Mary and Ann Laskey, who were also born in this village and were both rumoured to be over seven-foot tall.

'It's a churchyard of giants,' I whispered. 'They're everywhere.'

Nothing moved around us. Heath and I walked quietly, slightly on tiptoes, until we reached the gate.

'Do you think they still breed giants round here?' Heath asked, back on the road.

'Who knows? Have you even seen anyone?'

Heath shook his head. West Somerton was deserted. I had the feeling that inside the houses there might be more giants bent double in shadowy rooms, or snoring on reinforced beds. I kept it to myself that there's a trace of giants in my own family line, on my father's side. My great uncles were both touching seven-foot tall, and one of them was rumoured to have carried a pony back to his farm after it went lame. They had size fifteen boots standing in the hall, each with a row of nail heads hammered round the edges of the soles. 'You think they were big,' my father once said to me, alluding enigmatically to other giants in the family history. 'You should have seen the Blackburn women...'

We continued towards California and, at Hemsby, we walked alongside the twenty-two acre site of the abandoned Pontins Holiday Camp. By this time I was beginning to think the whole world was uninhabited, and that we'd inadvertently walked into a post-apocalyptic future where we were the only survivors. How had this happened, I thought? How had the world ended while we hadn't noticed? The Pontins camp was vast – it had once been able to accommodate two and a half thousand holidaymakers at a time, but now, only the bare outlines of its buildings, standing among knee-high weeds, could be seen beyond a chain-link fence.

'What would the aliens think, if they landed here?' Heath said, looking through the fence. 'With all those abandoned tennis courts and empty dance halls left to rot. They'd think humans must have given up trying to have fun.'

The holiday camp looked like a ghost town and – with its institutional architecture and geometric grid plan – bore an uncanny resemblance to Pripyat, the town next to Chernobyl hurriedly evacuated when the reactor exploded. I thought again of the photo of the doomed workers on the roof of Reactor 4, shovelling radioactive graphite, and wondered whether a similar catastrophe had happened here. Hemsby, twinned with Pripyat – I could imagine the sign. The streets in Pripyat are becoming forest once more. Nature abhors a vacuum, it moves in. Yet rooms in Pripyat's empty hospital still shimmer with a radioactive toxicity that has never been dealt with. And as I looked at the deserted Pontin's camp, at the weeds and trees that have begun to split open the concrete, it felt like an invisible radiation might be lurking there, also.

There are nearly two hundred lost villages in Norfolk, more than in most counties of England. Some of these villages were moved during the formation of the great estates. Others were shrunk as a result of plague or poverty, and a few were swept away by the sea. Shipden, off Cromer, was overrun by the waves in 1400, and the eroded stump of its church tower still lingers two hundred metres beyond the town pier. At Waxham Parva, the parish records end suddenly in 1383, when a storm surge destroyed the village. Further along the coast, the settlements of Wimpwell, Little Waxham, Ness, Clare and Foulness, were once thriving, but all of them were eventually lost to the sea. When the old church at Eccles was overrun by waves, its graveyard became scoured clean, exposing a group of skeletons that, in 1895, stared up at the sky for several days, before they were washed away.

Lost villages exert a special draw for me. I've mentioned elsewhere the morning I visited the Czech field where the village of Lidice once was, before it was eradicated by the Nazis in June 1942. It had felt indecent to walk across the grass where so much senseless pain had occurred. A new village of Lidice had been built, paid for by a British campaign, next to the field where the original one was destroyed. I remember wandering round this new village and feeling that the people living there would never be free of a share of tragedy. Their life was meant to neutralise a shadow, but it was the shadow that drew the light towards it. Similarly, in Herculaneum, under the brooding slopes of Vesuvius, I once stood in one of the excavated streets and, surrounded by the appearance of an intact town, had an overwhelming sense that around the corner there was a Roman child, sitting on the cobblestones. On the north coast of Cornwall I once visited the tiny harbour of Port Quin in the middle of the night, where all the men of the village had drowned in a freak storm after going to sea on the Sabbath. No one returned, the women and children became destitute, and the village was never lived in again. I stood on the shore that night, and was spooked by the inlet of water in front of me, and specifically the sound it made which was a little like a sigh, as if the sea carried a residual memory of what had happened there. At Masada in Israel, I looked down from the fortress walls and saw the giant ramp of earth the Roman besiegers had built to defeat the Sicarii zealots, and the ramp looked as fresh as if it had been made by bulldozers the day before. The past and present seemed joined in one moment, and I was afraid to look behind me in case the ground was covered with the nine hundred and sixty zealots who'd just slit their own throats, defiant even in death. And in the abandoned gold mining town of Ballarat – near Death Valley – I wandered around the ruins and finally came to the grave of its last resident, a man called Seldom Seen Slim, who'd lived on among the bare bricks for years after everyone else had left. He was one of the last of the single-blanket gold prospectors, and he must have known a great deal about what it was like to live among ghosts. On his grave was a simple inscription:

Me lonely? Hell no!

I'm half coyote and half wild burro.

Seldom Seen Slim

All these abandoned places share a lingering trace of the calamity that destroyed them, and often the disturbing speed with which they unravelled. And it's this speed – turning a thriving town into a ruin – that partly explains why these lost places resonate, and draw us towards them. Their unnerving message is that we're always only seconds away from catastrophe.

It's worth remembering: the universe is almost entirely made of oblivion.

In 1976, under a bed in Norwich, our dog Daisy gave birth to five puppies. It happened in the middle of the night, when births tend to occur, and my mother brought my brother and me into her bedroom to witness the event. The bedroom was calm, softly lit by a sidelight, and had an expectant quality I'd never seen in it before. There were no cars passing outside. Beneath the edge of the bed our dog was lying on her side, breathing heavily, trying to lift her neck as the pain of labour overtook her. My brother and I knelt on the floor while my mother delivered the puppies, each one emerging from

Daisy's pale white fur in a glistening purple sac, and inside each sac we saw the further miracle of a fully formed animal with legs bent double, wriggling slowly, nudging its way across the towel. The puppies began to explore the area cautiously, eyes half-closed, weakly stumbling. Daisy was – for that night – altered, not the scampering Jack Russell that ran down the pavements with a hind leg raised in the air. Here she was whimpering, and full of fear. There was the visceral smell of birth itself, acrid and hot – which to this day I can conjure up in all its vivid scent. Childhood can often seem like a foreign land, remembered in unreliable fragments – but there are events that seem to circumnavigate the wiring of memory itself, and the birth of those puppies is one of them. Five were born and, with each arrival, they were quickly named by my mother: Badger, Billy, Belle, Tinker and Barney. She ripped open the amniotic sac to release Belle, because even by this mid-point in the deliveries Daisy was too weak to do it. I think that tearing of the sac may have made a permanent connection with my mother, because Belle was the one we kept. The other four male pups were sent to various parts of the county, to family friends. Billy (the second born) was a good-looking puppy, full of life, although I only remember him as blunt-nosed, stumbling around on his soft paws, with a mewing voice and pin-sharp teeth. He went east, near to California, with a friend of my mother's from her college days. From the messages we received, he was a fun-loving dog, full of energy and loving a chase, until one day he sped over the grass after a rabbit and followed it down the hole. Billy got wedged in the maze of burrows somewhere below the ground, and he died in that tunnel.

I told Heath this story as we walked towards California, knowing that at any moment we might pass Billy's unmarked tomb under the grass, aware of a dog's life that had gone full circle, from the visceral slipperiness of his birth, to the dry tunnel of his death.

I realise now that this entire journey has been its own trip down a rabbit hole, where being lost has been more common than finding what I was looking for. Perhaps it's more interesting to lose your way, than to know exactly where you are? East Anglia is a warren of burrows full of wrong turns and dead ends and I've been following the scent of the trickster rabbit all this time. Sometimes I've felt close to catching what I was looking for. In the dark tunnels there have been the occasional scuffles, and I've briefly grabbed a pair of kicking hind legs and come away with a tuft of fur in my fingertips. But at other times I've crawled through the warren as the sandy soil falls in my eyes, with a doubtful feeling that I've been in this place before – and a moment later I see my own feet in front of me, wedged in the burrow. East Anglia, its essence, has remained just beyond my reach, where it belongs, in intangible fragments, in the scent of pine trees and sea salt in the Holkham woods, in the cool touch of knapped flint on a sunlit wall, in the fens' fading light where the shadow of dark soil seeps into the air. I've seen it in these places, I've seen it in my grandfather's photos and I've seen it in the people I've met along the way and the characters that have emerged. Fragments and visions, and as soon as I saw them, they were gone.

California

Heath and I walked past the road sign for California with mixed feelings. We were about to reach the end, but the journey behind us felt strangely beyond grasp. It seemed likely we'd end up with a similar attitude to the one we'd started with: more than a little confused about what we were actually looking for. The not quite visible; had we found it?

The road up to the village of California was straight, with a thick hedge on our right and a large holiday park spreading out across a field on our left. The individual holiday chalets were arranged among the grass in blocks and diamonds, like a game of Tetris being played by giants, where each rectangular chalet might slide through a gap and slot in alongside another while you weren't looking. I imagined newly arrived families on holiday: over-excited kids jumping up and down on beds, flushed with the sugar rush of change and possibility, while the parents wondered whether they were lost in some sort of mind-bending mathematical puzzle. In the middle of the night, these parents might look through their front windows and see a row of similar chalets and similar families, facing them. Where are we? How do we fit in here? How are we different from anyone else? I had the sense that marital problems might have aired themselves easily in this place. The chalet park looked charged, in fact, with relationship angst.

Heath wanted a closer look, so we left the road and began to take a meandering route through the chalets. We split up onto different paths, and I kept seeing him at various junctions, looking at the colours of front doors and, once, saw him crouching down by a garden gnome. He had Half-Shandy on a lead, and the dog looked up at me at one point with no sign of recognition. I stopped outside the frosted window of a bathroom, and noticed a flamboyant plastic flower arrangement pressed against it on the other side, as if there was a psychedelic jungle inside. Then, a short distance away, I came to an intersection of pathways, and was overwhelmed by the sheer quantity of geometric lines around me. Lost in the middle of the chalets, there was no view beyond, no horizon to say what was out there. It was a strange place to come for a holiday, I thought, to surround yourself with walls and geometry. Coming back to your room late at night must be daunting, especially if you'd been drinking, where the buildings might conspire into a maze of identical clapboard fronts and painted doors. Sticking out from several of the letterboxes were fliers for takeaway pizzas and burgers, and it occurred to me that memorising which letterboxes had these leaflets might be the best way to navigate the route in or out.

In the mini-market there was a smell of plastic beach balls and sun cream that I associate with childhood holidays to Spain. I stopped at a revolving cage of personalised miniature number plates that had names such as *Boy Racer, Girl Racer, Cool Chick, Cool Dude, Top Bloke, Football Crazy* and *No1 Teacher*. There was no one at the till, and it seemed to underline something that both of us were beginning to realise – there was no one here in California. Outside the shop, all we could hear was a 50p children's ride playing the theme to *Postman Pat*, while, next to it, a second ride was a child's space rocket pointing up towards the sky.

We carried on into the village itself, which didn't really have a centre, and was mostly a collection of more holiday homes built around a single car park. There was an amusements arcade and a chippy. We still hadn't seen anyone, and the village was beginning to resemble a ghost town. I fully expected the only person we might encounter would be Seldom Seen Slim, the lingering survivor of Ballarat, drawn to this place because it had a similar air for him to breathe. No one about, yet there still seemed to be a slightly aggressive vibe: the cars had been parked with very little space between them, and the layout of houses felt jostled and too close to each other. As with the chalet park, housing plots seemed to have been laid out in arbitrary triangles and squares, with virtually no fences to suggest where one house finished and the next began. Many of the buildings were made from a quirky mix of clapboard and tin roofs, with neglected porches and driveways. Among them was a bungalow that was particularly slumped and broken, sinking into a growing thicket of briars and nettles. The paint was flaked away, the shingles on the roof were buckled, and through one of the windows I saw a room with a collapsed ceiling, sprung floorboards and ivy growing up the wallpaper. When I walked round to the back I saw a glass porch, with an open fridge standing in the middle of the floor and, in a shadowy room behind it, a filthy mattress laid on plywood boards.

Oddly, next to this shack was another plot with a similar sized bungalow, but this one was maintained immaculately, with a close clipped lawn and a glossy front door. I was drawn to the join between the two building plots – where the feral mix of brambles and nettles on one side met a lawn which looked as neat as a carpet on the other, and in several places I could see the secateurs' marks on the briars, cut in a precise line hanging over the divide. I suppose the derelict shack was some sort of talking point in the village, a stain on the village's notion of what it should be, but for me I thought it added a deeper understanding of this place, the way a mad uncle can give an insight into the workings of an otherwise blandly respectable family.

Behind one of the bungalows I saw a flagpole, and hanging from it was the iconic grizzly bear and lone star design of the California state flag, with California Republic written clearly across it. I pointed it out to Heath. It was a satisfying sight – like finding the house in New York named *Brooklyn* – and seeing the flag fluttering in the breeze I felt like the whole journey had some sense of validity at last. We had, after all, managed to cross the East Anglian continent from New York to California, and the flag felt strangely as though it had been raised in our honour. We walked up to it, listened to it flapping in the breeze, and watched how the grizzly bear formed and reformed as the flag twisted.

We shook hands, congratulating each other, and shared a hug.

'We've done it, Heath,' I said. 'Did you think we'd make it?'

He shrugged. 'Is this the end point, then?'

'I don't know. It's as good as any.'

'I don't suppose we particularly need an end point, in any case. By the way – I don't remember a start point either.'

'I think it was –' I began, but realised someone was standing nearby trying to get our attention. *Excuse me* she kept saying. We both turned to see a woman in a raspberry coloured fleece standing at the back of her garden, staring at us.

'Can I ask you what you're doing?' she said in an east London accent, and a tone that wasn't friendly.

'We're looking at this,' Heath said, pointing at the flag.

'Do you know the people who live there?' she replied.

'No. Not at all.'

'So what are you up to?' She was standing in a section of the field that had been marked off as her back garden. A low picket fence, about three-feet high, was all there was to separate where she was and where we were, out in the field. By her feet was a sprightly little Yorkshire terrier, wagging its tail vigorously.

'Well – if you raise a flag, you're sort of expecting someone to look at it,' I said.

'It depends what you think about private property,' she said, beginning to walk away, wanting to have the last word on the matter. We looked around us. We were standing next to a public footpath, in a meadow. When she'd gone, the dog continued wagging its tail at us, as if saying: 'Don't mind her – she's on one.' Half-Shandy trotted forward and put his long nose through the gaps of the picket fence, and the Yorkshire terrier rocked from side to side, as if its tail was wagging the dog. Then the woman slid open a patio door and yelled for her dog to come in.

'Blimey,' I said, to Heath.

'Hardly Californian behaviour,' he said. We walked off, a little crestfallen that our moment of reaching the end had been interrupted.

'She had a point, I suppose,' Heath added. 'By asking us what we were up to. I mean – our whole journey – it's something neither of us has managed to answer properly.'

'Fair enough,' I said.

'Perhaps she sensed our fundamental problem – that we don't really know what we're doing here.'

'Either that, or she's just unpleasant.'

'More likely.'

We walked to the cliff edge and looked down on the beach, which was about thirty feet below us. It was deserted, with a line of soft waves breaking along the shore. This really was as far as we could walk to, without getting wet.

'Apparently, it's called California because gold coins kept getting found down there, on the beach,' I said. 'They'd been hidden in a well shaft, which broke open when the cliff eroded.'

'I see.'

'Heath, do you think we should've gone to America? We could have done the real journey?'

He thought about that. 'This is the real one,' he said. 'This is as real as any journey from New York to California.'

After a while, we turned to walk back, planning to call a cab to take us to Norwich, from where Heath would take the train to Cambridge and I'd head back to London, our journey over. I already felt confused about what we'd discovered, and daunted by the next stage of having to write about it. How could I possibly sum up this journey across the fens, along the coast and through the Broads, and expect it to convey anything other than a scratch on what I felt lay under the surface? I'd need some time off before I began, I thought. Let it settle into some sort of order, if there was any sort of order to be found. That's usually good advice for anything. Perhaps I'd start by hunting through my grandfather's photos of the fens, and see where they led. That seemed like a good place to start, because after all, that's where my journey started.

Across the meadow, I noticed a couple of benches had been placed overlooking the sea. There was no path leading to them and, as we approached, no scuff marks in the grass to show they'd ever been used. They looked as though they'd been dropped from the sky into the middle of the field, and had landed in a particularly windswept position. They must have been adjusted while their legs were set in concrete, with the benches angled towards each other a bit like an open hinge. It seemed a very deliberate angle that had been chosen, but not a particularly satisfying one.

They were a strange sight. The field was just too large, and the benches sat in a vacuum of air and sky and grass and sea that dwarfed them on all sides. I took a photo of them, walked back, took another photo to show how much field there was, then walked further back, until the benches were almost lost in the viewfinder.

I looked long and hard at these photos, wondering which one was most important to include in this book. Which one of them summed up the oddness of this place and the oddness of this journey that has repeatedly surprised me with all its many layers of oddness. Back home I stuck the photos on my kitchen wall and realised, in that moment, that it needed all three of them to form the image I was trying to capture. Together, they were the story. Three parting glances at a receding landscape.